ARIZONA BUCKET LIST

Set Off on **150 Epic Adventures** and Discover Incredible Destinations to Live Out Your Dreams While Creating Unforgettable Memories that Will Last a Lifetime.

(Online Digital MAP included - access it through the link provided in the MAP Chapter of this book)

BeCrePress Travel

ARIZONA BUCKET LIST

TABLE OF CONTENTS

ARIZONA BUCKET LIST

INTRODUCTION

Embark on a captivating journey through Arizona's stunning landscapes and vibrant culture with "150 Destinations: Explore the Splendors of Arizona." This comprehensive travel guide is a treasure trove of 150 must-visit destinations, each offering a unique experience that showcases the state's rich diversity.

This book covers everything from the iconic landmarks of the Grand Canyon and Sedona's red rock formations to the hidden gems in the Sonoran Desert and the charming historic towns sprinkled throughout. For each destination, you will find a detailed description, address, or Plus Code for easy navigation, nearby major cities, driving directions, ideal times to visit, access costs (if applicable), and GPS coordinates.

Additionally, the book features a bonus interactive map created by the author. Say goodbye to fumbling with maps or complicated apps – all the destinations are conveniently marked, ensuring seamless exploration.

Whether you are an adventurer seeking outdoor escapades, a history enthusiast yearning for cultural immersion, or a nature lover craving breathtaking vistas, "150 Destinations: Explore the Splendors of Arizona" is your gateway to unlocking the wonders Arizona offers. Prepare to embark on an unforgettable journey through the enchanting landscapes and hidden treasures of the Grand Canyon State.

ABOUT ARIZONA

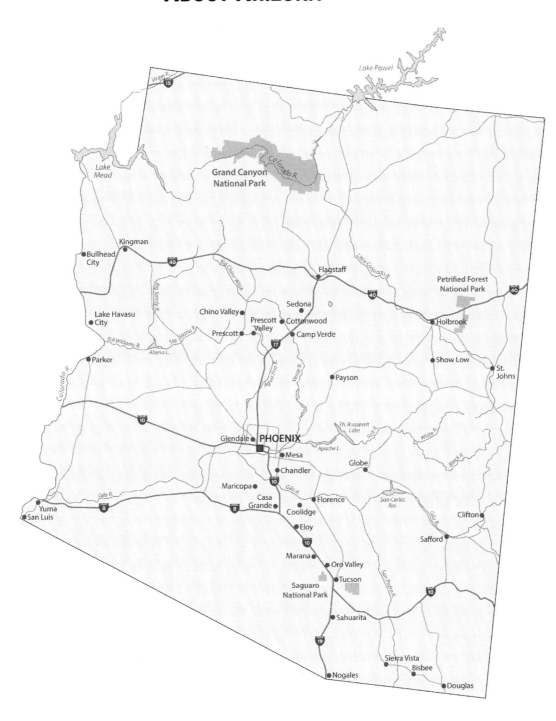

To access the Digital Map, please refer to the 'Map Chapter' in this book

Introduction

Welcome to the land of the Grand Canyon, Arizona! A state is known for its breathtaking natural beauty and unique culture. Arizona is famous for its diversity and has many attractions for everyone.

If you are a nature lover, you must have quality time here. If you are a passionate adventurer, there is plenty to explore. The southwestern United States of America is a world unto itself. Here you will see snow-covered mountains and crystal-clear lakes. In this chapter, we will take an overview of the Arizona. This chapter will guide you, and we will entice you on this fantastic journey of the diverse landscapes, flora and fauna, human settlements, outdoor recreation activities, and much more that make Arizona so unique!

Climate of Arizona

Arizona is famous for its desert climate, which makes it one of the hottest states in the US. The state has a dry environment with low humidity levels that can cause dehydration for people not used to such conditions.

During the summer, Arizona experiences high temperatures beyond 100 degrees Fahrenheit. You must stay indoors or carry sunscreen and water outside to avoid heat exhaustion or heat stroke.

However, Arizona's temperature drops drastically during winter, making it an excellent destination for people seeking mild weather during the cold season. Temperatures during this period typically fall within the 40 to 60 degrees Fahrenheit range.

The monsoon season in Arizona usually starts from June through September; this period comes with thunderstorms accompanied by heavy rainfalls that lead to flash floods and strong winds. These natural disasters may affect outdoor activities like hiking or camping hence be careful when planning your trip during these months.

Understanding Arizona's climate is crucial when visiting this beautiful state as it will help you plan accordingly based on your preferences and comfort level.

Landscape of Arizona

Arizona blesses with a diverse and unique landscape that mesmerizes tourists from all over the world. The state has everything from deserts, canyons, mountains, and plateaus to volcanic cones. It is no wonder that Arizona is called the "Grand Canyon State."

One of the most iconic landmarks in Arizona is the Grand Canyon; it is famous worldwide. It attracts a large number of visitors every year. The canyon stretches for 277 miles and reaches up to one mile deep. Its stunning red rocks are genuinely breathtaking.

Another famous landmark in Arizona is Monument Valley, located on Navajo land near the Utah border. This valley boasts towering sandstone formations carved by centuries of wind and rain erosion.

Arizona also has numerous mountain ranges, such as the San Francisco Peaks, which contain Humphreys Peak -the highest point in Arizona- while Camelback Mountain offers a popular hiking destination just outside Phoenix.

For those who want to experience something completely different, Antelope Canyon offers otherworldly views of smooth curves eroded into Navajo Sandstone by flash floods over time, creating an almost ethereal environment.

The Arizona landscape provides endless opportunities for exploration and adventure, making it an ideal place for outdoor enthusiasts or anyone looking to connect with nature.

Flora and Fauna

Arizona has a diverse flora and fauna due to its varied climate and landscape. The state's vegetation ranges from arid deserts filled with cacti to lush pine forests and deciduous trees.

In the desert regions, visitors can observe unique plant life, such as the iconic saguaro cactus, which can reach heights up to 40 feet tall! Other species include prickly pear cacti, creosote bush, and mesquite trees.

Moving into higher elevations brings about a completely different range of plant life. Aspens grow in groves at high altitudes, while towering ponderosa pines cover mountain slopes. In addition, Arizona boasts over 1,000 species of wildflowers that bloom throughout springtime.

The diverse ecosystems within Arizona also provide homes for countless animal species. Large mammals like elk and bighorn sheep roam amongst the mountains while smaller creatures like prairie dogs scurry through the grasslands.

Bird watchers will delight in spotting rare species, such as roadrunners or elegant trogons, among many others. Reptiles are abundant here, including rattlesnakes, lizards, and even Gila monsters!

It is clear that Arizona offers a rich experience when it comes to observing nature - adventurers will be satisfied with what they find here!

Natural Disasters

Arizona is no stranger to natural disasters, many of which occur frequently. One such disaster is wildfires, which often ravage large land areas and destroy homes and other properties. These fires are caused by lightning strikes or human negligence.

Another common natural disaster in Arizona is flash flooding, which occurs when heavy rains fall on dry soil that cannot absorb it quickly enough. It causes water to accumulate rapidly, leading to flooding that can cause significant damage to homes and infrastructure.

Droughts are also a significant concern in Arizona due to its arid climate. They can lead to crop failure, water shortages for humans and livestock, and an increased risk of wildfires.

In addition to these disasters, dust storms (haboobs) are another concern for Arizonans. These intense storms bring strong winds up to 60 miles per hour or more. The sand and dust they carry can severely reduce road visibility, making driving extremely hazardous.

ARIZONA BUCKET LIST

Arizona's geography makes it vulnerable to various types of natural disasters yearly. Residents and visitors must stay aware of weather conditions and take necessary precautions when traveling or living in the state.

Human Activities and Settlements

Human activities and settlements in Arizona have evolved from ancient indigenous communities to modern cities. When you visit Arizona, you observe that Native American tribes such as the Navajo, Hopi, and Apache have lived in the state for thousands of years, with their cultures still thriving today.

The arrival of European settlers brought about significant changes to the landscape and way of life. Mining booms like those in Tombstone and Jerome led to rapid population growth, while agriculture flourished thanks to irrigation projects.

Recently, Arizona has become home to bustling metropolitan areas like Phoenix and Tucson and smaller towns such as Sedona and Flagstaff, which are tourism hubs. The state's economy diversifies across healthcare, technology, and manufacturing industries.

Despite this development, Arizona has faced its fair share of challenges related to human activity. Water scarcity remains a major concern due to increased demand from a growing population and climate change impacts. In addition, urban sprawl has contributed to habitat loss for native species.

Efforts made by government agencies and conservation organizations alike to address these issues through sustainable land use practices, water management strategies, and wildlife conservation initiatives.

Outdoor Recreation and Tourism

Arizona is a famous destination for outdoor enthusiasts and tourists alike. With its diverse landscape, warm climate, and year-round sunshine, Arizona always has something to do throughout the year.

Arizona offers an array of world-renowned trails for hiking lovers that showcase some of America's most stunning natural landscapes. It is best either the Grand Canyon or Sedona's red rocks; countless opportunities exist to explore nature on foot.

Arizona has plenty of options if you are looking for water activities! The state boasts many beautiful lakes, such as Lake Powell and Lake Havasu, where visitors can enjoy boating, kayaking, or simply lounging on a sandy beach.

Camping is another favorite activity among Arizonans and visiting campers. With thousands of campsites scattered across National Parks like Petrified Forest or Saguaro National Park, campers can experience unique settings while enjoying all Mother Nature offers.

Lastly, golf courses are abundant throughout Arizona, making it a paradise for avid golfers who want to hit the links surrounded by breathtaking scenery at every turn!

Outdoor Recreation & Tourism is one of the main reasons people visit this beautiful state.

Conclusion

Arizona is a great state and one of the most beautiful places in America, with its diverse landscapes, unique flora and fauna, rich history, and thriving culture. It has something for everyone, whether you are an outdoor enthusiast looking forward to hiking through stunning natural scenery or a city dweller seeking bustling metropolises.

Despite being known for its scorching hot summers that can be challenging to cope with, Arizona remains an attractive destination throughout the year because of its many attractions and activities. There is always something new to discover, from world-class spas to local wineries, breweries, and excellent museums like Heard Museum.

If you intend to explore the southwest, nothing is better than Arizona. It offers plenty to everyone. This trip will increase precious memories—many worthy places like Grand Canyon National Park or historic towns like Tombstone. So pack your bags today and prepare yourself for an adventure filled with unforgettable memories!

Phoenix

1. Desert Botanical Garden

The Desert Botanical Garden is a stunning attraction in Phoenix, Arizona. Spanning over 140 acres, it showcases the remarkable diversity of desert plants worldwide. With more than 50,000 plant displays, including cacti, succulents, and other desert flora, the garden offers a mesmerizing experience for visitors. Its beautifully designed trails guide guests through themed gardens, highlighting the unique adaptations of desert plants to survive in arid environments. The park also hosts various events, exhibitions, and educational programs to promote conservation and appreciation of desert ecosystems. It serves as an oasis of natural beauty and knowledge, capturing the essence of the desert landscape.

Location: 1201 N Galvin Pkwy, Phoenix, AZ 85008, USA

Closest City or Town: Tempe, AZ **How to Get There:** To get to the Desert Botanical Garden in Phoenix, Arizona, drive to 1201 N Galvin Parkway or take public transportation to the nearby stop. Once there, purchase tickets and enjoy the diverse desert plant displays and breathtaking landscapes.

GPS Coordinates: 33.4615° N, 111.9441° W

Best Time to Visit: February-March

Pass/Permit/fees: The ticket costs $12-$25, while kids under 3 are free.

Did you Know? It is famous for its beauty and recreational activities.

2. Papago Park

Papago Park is a charming desert oasis over 1,200 acres. It is famous for its unique geological formations and stunning natural beauty; the park offers a range of recreational activities and attractions. Visitors can explore the picturesque hiking and biking trails, enjoy picnics in the shaded ramadas, or marvel at the iconic Hole-in-the-Rock formation with its panoramic city views. The park becomes home to the Phoenix Zoo, the Desert Botanical Garden, and the Papago Golf Course, providing ample opportunities for entertainment and relaxation. Papago Park truly encapsulates the enchanting spirit of the Arizona desert.

Location: 625 N Galvin Pkwy, Phoenix, AZ 85008, USA

Closest City or Town: Messa, AZ

How to Get There: To get to Papago Park in Phoenix, Arizona, drive to the park's entrances off Galvin Parkway or McDowell Road, or take public transportation to the nearby stops.

GPS Coordinates: 33.4536° N, 111.9487° W

Best Time to Visit: November-April

Pass/Permit/fees: Entry is free.

Did you Know? It is a home of hiking trails, picnic areas, and the iconic Hole-in-the-Rock formation.

3. Piestewa Peak

Piestewa Peak, also famous as Squaw Peak, is a historical landmark and popular hiking destination in Phoenix, Arizona. Rising to an elevation of 2,608 feet, it offers breathtaking views of the nearest desert landscape. The peak is named in honor of brave woman Lori Piestewa, the first Native American woman to die in combat for the USA. Hikers can challenge themselves on well-maintained trails, such as the Summit Trail, which rewards climbers with stunning vistas at the top. Piestewa Peak is a natural gem symbol of courage and resilience, attracting outdoor enthusiasts and visitors alike.

Location: Phoenix, AZ 85016, USA

Closest City or Town: Scottsdale, AZ

How to Get There: To get to Piestewa Peak in Phoenix, Arizona, drive to the parking area off Squaw Peak Drive or take the Valley Metro bus route 56 to Lincoln Drive.

GPS Coordinates: 33.5474° N, 112.0208° W

Best Time to Visit: October-March

Pass/Permit/fees: Per family, $115.

Did you Know? You can enjoy panoramic views of the city and desert landscape.

4. Children's Museum of Phoenix

The Children's Museum of Phoenix is a vibrant and interactive educational destination explicitly designed for children. Located in Phoenix, Arizona, it offers a multitude of hands-on exhibits and activities that spark curiosity and ignite the imagination. From exploring the noodle forest and constructing with blocks to experimenting with water and engaging in imaginative play, children immerse in learning and discovery. The museum also hosts special events, workshops, and programs for different age groups. With its welcoming and engaging environment, the Children's Museum of Phoenix provides a fun and enriching experience for young minds to explore, create, and grow.

Location: 215 N 7th St, Phoenix, AZ 85034, USA

Closest City or Town: Peoria, AZ

How to Get There: Head to 215 N 7th Street in downtown Phoenix by car or public transportation to the Children's Museum of Phoenix.

GPS Coordinates: 33.4504° N, 112.0646° W

Best Time to Visit: November-April

Pass/Permit/fees: The ticket costs $13-$15, while kids under 1 are free.

Did you Know? Children may have interactive exhibits, hands-on activities, learning, and creativity here.

5. Musical Instrument Museum

The Musical Instrument Museum (MIM) is a captivating institution celebrating the universal language of music through an impressive collection of over 15,000 instruments worldwide. MIM offers visitors an immersive and educational experience located in Phoenix, Arizona. The museum showcases tools from around the globe, representing diverse cultures and traditions. Each exhibit features beautifully crafted puppets accompanied by multimedia presentations that bring the sounds and stories behind them to life. From ancient relics to modern marvels, MIM offers a comprehensive exploration of musical heritage. It is a must-visit destination for music enthusiasts and cultural explorers, with interactive displays, live performances, and engaging workshops.

Location: 4725 E Mayo Blvd, Phoenix, AZ 85050, USA

Closest City or Town: Sun City

How to Get There: To visit the Musical Instrument Museum (MIM), plan your trip to Phoenix, Arizona, and purchase tickets online or at the ticket counter.

GPS Coordinates: 33.6680° N, 111.9783° W

Best Time to Visit: Throughout the year

Pass/Permit/fees: The ticket costs $10-$20.

Did you Know? You can explore the diverse collection of instruments and enjoy live performances and interactive exhibits.

6.   Hall of Flame Museum of Firefighting

The Hall of Flame Museum of Firefighting, located in Phoenix, Arizona, is a remarkable institution dedicated to preserving the rich history of firefighting. With a collection of over 100 years, the museum showcases a vast array of firefighting equipment, antique fire engines, and artifacts. Visitors can explore interactive exhibits highlighting the evolution of firefighting techniques and the bravery of firefighters throughout history. From hand-drawn pumps to modern fire trucks, the museum offers a captivating glimpse into the world of firefighting. Educational programs, guided tours, and engaging displays make the Hall of Flame Museum a must-visit destination for fire service professionals and enthusiasts.

Location: 6101 E Van Buren St, Phoenix, AZ 85008, USA

Closest City or Town: Peoria, AZ

How to Get There: To reach the Hall of Flame Museum of Firefighting in Phoenix, Arizona, head to 6101 E Van Buren St and explore the extensive collection of firefighting equipment and artifacts.

GPS Coordinates: 33.4477° N, 111.9533° W

Best Time to Visit: Summer, Fall

Pass/Permit/fees: The ticket costs $17.

Did you Know? You may view the rich history of firefighting through interactive exhibits and displays.

7.   Echo Canyon Trail and Recreation Area

Echo Canyon Trail and Recreation Area, located in Phoenix, Arizona, offers nature and hiking enthusiasts an exhilarating outdoor experience. The trail, known for its challenging ascent to the summit of Camelback Mountain, provides breathtaking panoramic views of the surrounding desert landscape. Hikers can traverse rugged terrain, encounter unique rock formations, and marvel at the diverse flora and fauna. While the trail can be steep and demanding, the rewarding views at the top make it all worthwhile. With its stunning vistas and stimulating adventure, Echo Canyon Trail is a must-visit destination for those seeking an unforgettable outdoor excursion.

Location: 4925 E McDonald Dr, Phoenix, AZ 85018, USA

Closest City or Town: Glendale, AZ

How to Get There: To reach the Echo Canyon Trail and Recreation Area, travel to Phoenix, Arizona, and locate the trailhead at Camelback Mountain.

GPS Coordinates: 33.5226° N , 111.9751° W

Best Time to Visit: Summer

Pass/Permit/fees: Different packages are available.

Did you Know? It is a place for hikers and adventurers.

8.   Orpheum Theater

The Orpheum Theater is a historic cultural landmark in downtown Phoenix, Arizona. Built in 1929, the theatre showcases stunning Spanish Baroque Revival architecture and ornate detailing. Its grand interior boasts a lavish auditorium adorned with intricate chandeliers, decorative plasterwork, and a beautiful proscenium arch. The Orpheum Theater has hosted many performances, including Broadway shows, concerts, ballets, and more. After undergoing extensive restoration, the theatre continues to be a vibrant hub for arts and entertainment, captivating audiences with its timeless beauty and offering diverse cultural experiences to the community and visitors alike.

Location: 203 W Adams St, Phoenix, AZ 85003, USA

Closest City or Town: Scottsdale, AZ

How to Get There: Visitors can reach the theatre by car, public transportation, or rideshare.

GPS Coordinates: 33.4492° N, 112.0767° W

Best Time to Visit: Throughout the year.

Pass/Permit/fees: The ticket costs $48-$98.

Did you Know? It is famous for its vibrant arts and entertainment scene.

9.   Heard Museum

The Heard Museum, located in Phoenix, Arizona, is a renowned institution dedicated to preserving and showcasing the art, culture, and history of Native American peoples. Established in 1929, the museum houses an extensive collection of Native American artifacts, including textiles, pottery, jewelry, and contemporary art. With its engaging exhibitions, educational programs, and special events, the Heard Museum offers visitors a deep understanding and appreciation of Native American heritage. The museum's stunning architecture and serene outdoor spaces further enhance the experience, providing a tranquil environment to reflect upon the rich and diverse traditions of Native American cultures.

Location: 2301 N Central Ave, Phoenix, AZ 85004, USA

Closest City or Town: Tempe, AZ

How to Get There: The Heard Museum is at 2301 N Central Ave, Phoenix, AZ 85004, in central Phoenix, just north of downtown. Visitors can access the museum by driving and utilizing the on-site parking facilities. Alternatively, they can use public transportation with the nearest light rail station Encanto/Central Ave, or ride-sharing services to conveniently reach the museum.

GPS Coordinates: 33.4726° N, 112.0722° W

Best Time to Visit: February.

Pass/Permit/fees: The ticket costs $7-$18. Kids under 5 are free.

Did you Know? It is a home of diverse traditions and cultures.

10.   Camelback Mountain

Camelback Mountain in Phoenix, Arizona, is a prominent landmark and popular destination for outdoor enthusiasts. Its distinctive shape resembling the hump and head of a camel makes it a recognizable feature of the city skyline. The mountain offers breathtaking panoramic views of the surrounding desert landscape. Hiking trails, including the challenging Echo Canyon Trail and the more moderate Cholla Trail, attract visitors seeking adventure and a rewarding climb. With its unique geological formations and abundant flora and fauna, Camelback Mountain is a treasured natural gem providing recreational opportunities and natural beauty.

Location: Phoenix, AZ 85018, United States

Closest City or Town: Mesa, AZ

How to Get There: To get to Camelback Mountain in Phoenix, Arizona, choose the Echo Canyon Trailhead or Cholla Trailhead and follow directions to the respective parking areas. Be prepared with proper hiking gear and arrive early to secure parking, as both trailheads have limited space.

GPS Coordinates: 33.5151° N, 111.9619° W

Best Time to Visit: May- October

Pass/Permit/fees: Different packages are available online.

Did you Know? It is famous for its natural beauty and breathtaking views.

11. Chase Field

Chase Field, located in downtown Phoenix, Arizona, is a renowned sports stadium and home to Major League Baseball's Arizona Diamondbacks. Opened in 1998, the stadium offers baseball fans a modern and comfortable environment. Its retractable roof and air conditioning system ensures a comfortable experience regardless of the desert climate. With a seating capacity of over 48,500, Chase Field has hosted many memorable events, including All-Star Games and postseason matchups. The stadium also features unique amenities like a swimming pool and a centerfield party deck, adding to the excitement and entertainment value of attending a game at this iconic venue.

Location: 401 E Jefferson St, Phoenix, AZ 85004, USA

Closest City or Town: Tempe, AZ

How to Get There: Head to Chase Field in downtown Phoenix. Utilize nearby parking facilities or consider using public transportation or rideshare services for convenient access to the stadium.

GPS Coordinates: 33.4453° N, 112.0667° W

Best Time to Visit: Spring, Fall

Pass/Permit/fees: The ticket costs $40.

Did you Know? It is a hub of games.

12. South Mountain Park

South Mountain Park is a sprawling natural sanctuary in Phoenix, Arizona. Spanning over 16,000 acres, it is one of the biggest and finest municipal parks in the United States. This desert oasis offers visitors a mesmerizing blend of rugged beauty and outdoor recreational opportunities. With its vast network of trails, hikers, bikers, and horseback riders can explore the park's scenic vistas, towering saguaro cacti, and diverse wildlife. The park is also home to archaeological sites that showcase the rich history of the region's indigenous peoples.

Location: 10919 S Central Ave, Phoenix, AZ 85042, USA

Closest City or Town: Glendale, AZ

How to Get There: Visitors can be reached by taking Interstate 10 and exiting onto Baseline Road or utilizing public transportation or ride-sharing services for convenient access.

GPS Coordinates: 33.3403° N, 112.0609° W

Best Time to Visit: April-June

Pass/Permit/fees: Entry is free.

Did you Know? It is a captivating destination that embraces the splendor of the Sonoran Desert.

13. Hole in the Rock

Hole in the Rock is a unique geological formation in Papago Park, Phoenix, Arizona. This natural marvel draws visitors with its captivating beauty and intriguing history. The sandstone butte features a distinctive opening that leads to an expansive chamber with breathtaking views of the surrounding landscape. This iconic landmark holds cultural significance to the Native American tribes of the area, who consider it sacred. Tourists can hike to the top of the butte and explore the chamber, witnessing stunning sunsets and panoramic vistas.

Location: 625 N Galvin Pkwy, Phoenix, AZ 85008, USA

Closest City or Town: Avondale, AZ

How to Get There: Hole in the Rock is accessible by car via Interstate 10 and 52nd Street or by utilizing public transportation or ride-sharing services for convenient access.

GPS Coordinates: 33.4565° N, 111.9453° W

Best Time to Visit: Spring, Fall

Pass/Permit/fees: The ticket costs $5-$10. Kids under 5 are free.

Did you Know? It is a natural wonder and a connection to Arizona's rich heritage.

14. Phoenix Art Museum

The Phoenix Art Museum is a vibrant cultural hub in the heart of Phoenix, Arizona. Spanning more than 285,000 square feet, the museum offers a diverse collection of art spanning centuries and continents. From ancient artifacts to modern masterpieces, visitors can explore a range of artistic expressions across various mediums. The museum showcases renowned works by artists such as Frida Kahlo, Georgia O'Keeffe, and Diego Rivera. Additionally, it hosts rotating exhibitions, educational programs, and engaging events celebrating human expression's beauty and creativity.

Location: 1625 N Central Ave, Phoenix, AZ 85004, USA

Closest City or Town: Peoria, AZ

How to Get There: Phoenix Art Museum in Phoenix, Arizona, can be reached by car via Interstate 10 and McDowell Road or by utilizing public transportation or ride-sharing services for convenient access.

GPS Coordinates: 33.4671° N, 112.0728° W

Best Time to Visit: April-November

Pass/Permit/fees: General entry is free.

Did you Know? It is a must-visit destination for art enthusiasts and curious minds alike.

15. St. Mary's Basilica

St. Mary's Basilica, situated in downtown Phoenix, Arizona, is a magnificent religious landmark and a testament to Gothic Revival architecture. It's soaring spires and intricate stained glass windows captivate the eyes and hearts of visitors. The basilica, built in the late 19th century, holds a rich history and serves as the oldest Catholic parish in Phoenix. The grandeur continues with ornate altars, intricate woodwork, and a stunning pipe organ inside. St. Mary's Basilica stands as a symbol of faith, beauty, and community, welcoming all who seek solace, inspiration, or wish to admire its awe-inspiring craftsmanship.

Location: 231 N 3rd St, Phoenix, AZ 85004, USA

Closest City or Town: Peoria, AZ

How to Get There: To reach St. Mary's Basilica in downtown Phoenix, Arizona, drive north on 7th Avenue from the I-10 freeway until you reach Monroe Street. The basilica will be on your left at the intersection of 7th Avenue and Monroe Street. Alternatively, you can take the Valley Metro Light Rail to the Van Buren/Central Avenue station and walk a short distance to the basilica.

GPS Coordinates: 33.4506° N, 112.0698° W

Best Time to Visit: Spring, Summer

Pass/Permit/fees: You can book tickets online.

Did you Know? It is a home of craftsmanship.

GLENDALE

1.   State Farm Stadium

State Farm Stadium is a premier sports and entertainment venue renowned for its grandeur and modern amenities. As the home stadium of the NFL's Arizona Cardinals, it boasts a seating capacity of over 63,000 and a retractable roof, ensuring an unforgettable game-day experience. Beyond football, the stadium has hosted numerous marquee events, including Super Bowl games and major concerts. Its state-of-the-art facilities, expansive concourses, and advanced technology create an immersive environment for fans.

Location: 1 Cardinals Dr, Glendale, AZ 85305, USA

Closest City or Town: California

How to Get There: It can be reached by car via Loop 101 and exiting onto Bethany Home Road or Glendale Avenue or by utilizing public transportation or ride-sharing services for convenient access.

GPS Coordinates: 33.5276° N, 112.2626° W

Best Time to Visit: Throughout the year

Pass/Permit/fees: Different packages are available online.

Did you Know? It is a home of sports and entertainment.

SCOTTSDALE

1. Western Spirit: Scottsdale's Museum of the West

Scottsdale's Museum of the West is a captivating cultural institution in Scottsdale, Arizona. This unique museum celebrates the rich heritage and history of the American West through its engaging exhibits and immersive experiences. Visitors can explore the art, artifacts, and stories that depict the diverse landscapes, peoples, and events that shaped the West. From Native American artwork to cowboy culture, the museum offers a comprehensive view of the region's past and present.

Location: 3830 N Marshall Way, Scottsdale, AZ 85251, USA

Closest City or Town: Paradise Valley, AZ

How to Get There: It can be accessed by car via Loop 101 and Indian School Road or by utilizing public transportation or ride-sharing services for convenient access.

GPS Coordinates: 33.4921° N, 111.9284° W

Best Time to Visit: Throughout the year

Pass/Permit/fees: $25 for the yearly membership.

Did you Know? It is famous for its stunning architecture and thoughtfully curated displays.

2. Scottsdale Fashion Square

Scottsdale Fashion Square is a premier shopping destination in Scottsdale, Arizona. Its luxurious ambiance and extensive selection of high-end fashion brands offer a sophisticated retail experience. Spanning over 2 million square feet, the mall houses an array of upscale boutiques, department stores, and designer shops, catering to fashion enthusiasts and discerning shoppers. Beyond fashion, the complex boasts a variety of dining options, entertainment venues, and art installations, ensuring a well-rounded experience.

Location: 7014 E Camelback Rd, Scottsdale, AZ 85251, USA

Closest City or Town: Tempe, AZ

How to Get There: Visitors can access by car via Loop 101 and Scottsdale Road or by utilizing public transportation or ride-sharing services for convenient access.

GPS Coordinates: 33.5028° N, 111.9293° W

Best Time to Visit: Throughout the year

Pass/Permit/fees: $17.50.

Did you Know? It is a home of exquisite style, exclusive offerings, and a vibrant atmosphere.

3. Tom's Thumb Trailhead

Tom's Thumb Trailhead is a popular hiking destination in the McDowell Sonoran Preserve in Scottsdale. It offers breathtaking desert scenery and stunning panoramic views, and this trailhead is a paradise for outdoor enthusiasts. The trailhead is the starting point for several exhilarating trails, including the iconic Tom's Thumb Trail. As hikers embark on their journey, they treat to a diverse landscape of rugged mountains, towering saguaro cacti, and unique rock formations. The challenging yet rewarding ascent to Tom's Thumb rewards adventurers with a majestic granite spire and the beauty and grandeur of the Arizona wilderness.

Location: Scottsdale, AZ 85255, USA

Closest City or Town: Mesa, AZ · Phoenix, AZ · Gilbert, AZ ; Fountain Hills, AZ · Chandler, AZ · Glendale, AZ

How to Get There: Visitors can Drive east on East Shea Boulevard and turn right onto North 124th Street. Continue on East Ranch Gate Road until you reach the entrance of the McDowell Sonoran Preserve.

GPS Coordinates: 33.6945° N, 111.8017° W

Best Time to Visit: Throughout the year

Pass/Permit/fees: Different packages are available.

Did you Know? It is famous for its beauty and hiking trails.

4.   Taliesin West

Taliesin West is an architectural masterpiece and a historic landmark in Scottsdale, Arizona. Renowned architect Frank Lloyd Wright designed it as his winter home, studio, and architectural school. This desert sanctuary showcases Wright's theoretical principles, seamlessly blending with the natural surroundings. The organic architecture, incorporating local materials and innovative

design, harmonizes with the rugged Sonoran Desert landscape. Visitors can explore the distinctive structures, including the iconic drafting studio and living quarters, gaining insight into Wright's creative process and profound influence on American architecture.

Location: 12621 N Frank Lloyd Wright Blvd, Scottsdale, AZ 85259, USA

Closest City or Town: Mesa, AZ

How to Get There: Drive north on North Scottsdale Road and turn left onto East Cactus Road. Continue on East Cactus Road until you reach North Frank Lloyd Wright Boulevard, then turn right. Follow North Frank Lloyd Wright Boulevard until you reach Taliesin West Road, and turn left to arrive at the entrance of Taliesin West.

GPS Coordinates: 33.6064° N, 111.8452° W

Best Time to Visit: Throughout the year

Pass/Permit/fees: The ticket costs $25-$50.

Did you Know? It is famous for its stunning architecture.

5.   Penske Racing Museum

The Penske Racing Museum is a must-visit attraction for motorsport enthusiasts in Scottsdale, Arizona. Celebrating the legacy of the legendary Penske Racing Team, the museum offers a captivating display of race cars, trophies, and memorabilia from decades of racing history. Visitors can explore the meticulously restored vehicles, including iconic Indy cars and NASCAR machines that have conquered prestigious races. The museum also showcases the remarkable achievements of the Penske team, highlighting their dominance in various racing series. With interactive exhibits and informative displays, the Penske Racing

Museum provides an immersive experience that captures the thrill and excitement of motorsports.

Location: 7125 E Chauncey Ln, Phoenix, AZ 85054, USA

Closest City or Town: Phoenix, AZ

How to Get There: To reach the Penske Racing Museum in Scottsdale, Arizona, drive north on North Scottsdale Road and turn left onto East Princess Drive. Continue on East Princess Drive until you reach North Hayden Road, then turn right. Follow North Hayden Road until you reach the Penske Racing Museum at 7125 East Chauncey Lane.

GPS Coordinates: 33.6509° N, 111.9266° W

Best Time to Visit: Summer, Fall

Pass/Permit/fees: The ticket costs $99.

Did you Know? It is a home of motorsports, and plenty to enjoy here.

6. Butterfly Wonderland

Butterfly Wonderland is a captivating destination that offers a mesmerizing experience for nature lovers of all ages. This expansive indoor butterfly conservatory is home to thousands of vibrant butterflies worldwide. Visitors can immerse themselves in the lush tropical rainforest environment and witness the enchanting beauty of these delicate creatures in flight. With interactive exhibits, educational displays, and knowledgeable staff, Butterfly Wonderland provides a unique opportunity to learn about the butterflies life cycle, behavior, and conservation. It is a magical place where visitors can experience the wonders of nature up close and create unforgettable memories.

Location: 9500 East Vía de Ventura F100, Scottsdale, AZ 85256, USA

Closest City or Town: Gilbert, AZ

How to Get There: To get to Butterfly Wonderland in Scottsdale, Arizona, drive east on East Indian Bend Road and turn left onto North Hayden Road. Continue on North Hayden Road until you reach the OdySea in the Desert complex at 9500 East Vía de Ventura.

GPS Coordinates: 33.5545° N, 111.8762° W

Best Time to Visit: Throughout the year.

Pass/Permit/fees: The ticket costs $44. Kids under 2 are free.

Did you Know? It is famous for its butterfly wonderland.

7. McCormick-Stillman Railroad Park

McCormick-Stillman Railroad Park, situated in Scottsdale, is a beloved recreational destination that delights visitors of all ages. This expansive park pays homage to the rich history of railroads with its impressive collection of meticulously restored vintage locomotives and carriages. Visitors can take a leisurely ride on the Paradise & Pacific Railroad, a charming miniature train that winds through the park's scenic landscape. The park also features a carousel, a playground, picnic areas, and a museum, providing endless entertainment options. McCormick-Stillman Railroad Park is a true gem where families can create cherished memories and immerse themselves in the timeless allure of trains.

Location: 7301 E Indian Bend Rd, Scottsdale, AZ 85250, USA

Closest City or Town: Fountain Hills

How to Get There: Drive east on East Indian Bend Road and turn left onto North Hayden Road. Continue on North Hayden Road until you reach the park entrance located at 7301 East Indian Bend Road.

GPS Coordinates: 33.5371° N, 111.9233° W

Best Time to Visit: Summer, Fall.

Pass/Permit/fees: Entry is free.

Did you Know? You can enjoy the railroad experience and activities.

8.   McDowell Sonoran Preserve

The McDowell Sonoran Preserve is a natural gem in Scottsdale, Arizona's heart. This vast preserve offers a stunning display of desert landscapes, rugged mountains, and diverse wildlife. It serves as a sanctuary for countless plant and animal species, including iconic saguaro cacti and elusive desert bighorn sheep. The preserve is a haven for outdoor enthusiasts, boasting an extensive network of hiking, biking, and equestrian trails that wind through picturesque canyons and valleys. Visitors can immerse themselves in the tranquillity of the Sonoran Desert, marvel at breathtaking sunsets, and experience the timeless beauty of nature at its finest.

Location: 18333 N Thompson Peak Pkwy, Scottsdale, AZ 85255, United States

Closest City or Town: Chandler, AZ

How to Get There: To access the McDowell Sonoran Preserve, drive to one of the trailheads, such as the Gateway Trailhead at 18333 N Thompson Peak Pkwy, Scottsdale, AZ. Check the preserve's website for directions and parking information. Public transportation or biking/walking are also options, depending on your location and preference.

GPS Coordinates: 33.6494° N, 111.8585° W

Best Time to Visit: Summer, Spring

Pass/Permit/fees: The ticket costs $25- $50.

Did you Know? It is famous for its beauty and several outdoor activities.

9.   Southwest Wildlife Conservation Center

The Southwest Wildlife Conservation Center (SWCC) is a remarkable sanctuary in Scottsdale, Arizona. Covering 160 acres, SWCC dedicates to rescuing and rehabilitating native wildlife, focusing on injured, orphaned, or displaced animals. This non-profit organization provides a haven for many species, including coyotes, bobcats, bears, mountain lions, etc. SWCC's dedicated professionals and volunteers tirelessly offer veterinary care, habitat restoration, and educational programs to promote wildlife conservation. Visitors can tour the center, witness awe-inspiring wildlife up close, and learn about the importance of preserving and protecting these magnificent creatures.

Location: 27026 N 156th St, Scottsdale, AZ 85262, USA

Closest City or Town: Glendale, AZ

How to Get There: To reach the Southwest Wildlife Conservation Center (SWCC) in Scottsdale, Arizona, drive to 27026 N 156th Street. Public transportation options are limited, so it is recommended to use a car or taxi service.

GPS Coordinates: 33.7315° N, 111.7468° W

Best Time to Visit: Summer, Fall

Pass/Permit/fees: The ticket costs $30.Kids under 3 are free.

Did you Know? It is a home of wildlife.

10. Pinnacle Peak Park

Pinnacle Peak Park is a breathtaking natural landmark in Scottsdale, Arizona. This 150-acre desert preserve offers a captivating hiking experience with its iconic granite peak at 3,169 feet. Visitors can embark on well-maintained trails that wind through the picturesque Sonoran Desert, showcasing stunning vistas, unique rock formations, and abundant desert flora and fauna. The park is known for its diverse wildlife, including desert tortoises, javelinas, and numerous bird species. Whether you are a seasoned hiker or a nature enthusiast, Pinnacle Peak Park provides a serene escape and an opportunity to immerse yourself in the rugged beauty of the Arizona desert.

Location: 26802 N 102nd Way, Scottsdale, AZ 85262, USA

Closest City or Town: Glendale, AZ

How to Get There: To reach Pinnacle Peak Park in Scottsdale, Arizona, drive to 26802 N 102nd Way. Public transportation options are limited, so a car or taxi service is recommended.

GPS Coordinates: 33.7279° N, 111.8604° W

Best Time to Visit: Throughout the year

Pass/Permit/fees: The ticket costs $25-$100.

Did you Know? It is a home of wildlife and desert flora and fauna.

MESA

1. Organ Stop Pizza

Organ Stop Pizza is a unique dining experience in Mesa, Arizona. It combines the deliciousness of pizza with the mesmerizing sounds of a magnificent Wurlitzer organ. As you indulge in mouthwatering pizzas, pasta, and salads, you will entertain by talented organists who skillfully play the largest Wurlitzer pipe organ in the world. The great instrument boasts over 5,500 pipes, creating a captivating symphony of music. The nostalgic ambiance, tasty food, and incredible live organ performances make Organ Stop Pizza a must-visit destination for pizza lovers and music enthusiasts seeking a truly unforgettable dining experience.

Location: 1149 E Southern Ave, Mesa, AZ 85204, USA

Closest City or Town: Gilbert, AZ

How to Get There: To reach Organ Stop Pizza in Mesa, Arizona, drive to 1149 E Southern Ave.

Public transportation options are available but may require multiple transfers.

GPS Coordinates: 33.3929° N, 111.8078° W

Best Time to Visit: Throughout the year

Pass/Permit/fees: Entry is free.

Did you Know? It is an ideal place for Pizza lovers.

2. Usery Mountain Regional Park

Usery Mountain Regional Park is a stunning natural gem in Mesa, Arizona. This park offers a wealth of outdoor recreational activities and breathtaking desert landscapes. Visitors can explore numerous hiking trails, showcasing the beauty of the Sonoran Desert, with panoramic views of the surrounding mountains. The park is also home to various plant and animal species, making it a haven for nature enthusiasts and wildlife lovers. With picnic areas, camping facilities, and opportunities for birdwatching and stargazing, Usery Mountain Regional Park provides a serene escape and a chance to connect with the tranquility of the desert.

Location: 3939 N Usery Pass Rd, Mesa, AZ 85207, USA

Closest City or Town: Tempe, AZ · Chandler, AZ · Scottsdale, AZ · Paradise Valley, AZ ·

How to Get There: To reach Usery Mountain Regional Park in Mesa, Arizona, drive to 3939 N Usery Pass Road. Public transportation options are limited, so a car or taxi service is recommended.

GPS Coordinates: 33.4792° N, 111.6195° W

Best Time to Visit: Summer, Spring

Pass/Permit/fees: The ticket costs $7.

Did you Know? It is famous for wildlife and plants.

3.   Commemorative Air Force Airbase Arizona Museum

The Commemorative Air Force (CAF) Airbase Arizona Museum is a stunning tribute to aviation history and an immersive experience for enthusiasts and visitors alike. Located in Mesa, Arizona, this extraordinary museum showcases an impressive collection of vintage military aircraft that have been meticulously restored to their former glory. Stepping into the museum feels like stepping back in time, with iconic aircraft such as the B-17 Flying Fortress, P-51 Mustang, and B-25 Mitchell on display. The knowledgeable volunteers and guides share stories of courage and heroism, providing valuable insight into the aircraft's significance and the brave individuals who flew them.

Location: 2017 N Greenfield Rd, Mesa, AZ 85215, USA

Closest City or Town: Chandler, AZ

How to Get There: To reach the Commemorative Air Force Airbase Arizona Museum in Mesa, Arizona, enter the 2017 N Greenfield Rd address into your GPS or navigation app. If using public transportation, check for nearby bus routes or consider using a taxi or ride-sharing service.

GPS Coordinates: 33.4169° N , 111.6867° W

Best Time to Visit: Throughout the year.

Pass/Permit/fees: The ticket costs $5-$15.

Did you Know? You can observe the remarkable legacy of aviation history.

4.   Mesa Temple & Visitors' Center

The Mesa Temple & Visitors' Center is a cherished landmark in Mesa, Arizona. It holds significant spiritual and historical importance as one of the ancient operating temples of The Church of Jesus Christ of Latter-day Saints. The temple's stunning architecture and beautifully manicured grounds make it a sight to behold. The Visitor Center offers informative exhibits, interactive displays, and friendly volunteers who share the history and beliefs of the Church. Whether you seek a peaceful retreat, religious insight, or appreciate architectural marvels, the Mesa Temple & Visitors' Center provides a serene and enlightening experience for all who visit.

Location: 455 E Main St, Mesa, AZ 85203, USA

Closest City or Town: Scottsdale, AZ

How to Get There: To reach the Mesa Temple & Visitors' Center in Mesa, Arizona, head towards the intersection of Main Street and Mesa Drive. Input the address 525 East Main Street into your GPS or navigation app for precise directions.

GPS Coordinates: 33.4149° N, 111.8207° W

Best Time to Visit: Throughout the year.

Pass/Permit/fees: Entry is free but requires a reservation.

Did you Know? It is a stunning place for photography.

5.   Mesa Arts Center

Arizona's Mesa Arts Center is a vibrant hub for creativity and cultural enrichment. This sprawling facility in downtown Mesa encompasses four theaters, several art galleries, and numerous studio spaces. It hosts an eclectic range of performances, including theater, dance, music, and comedy, attracting local talent and renowned artists worldwide. The center is a hub of educational programs, workshops, and community events, fostering artistic development and engagement with its innovative architecture, dynamic programming, and commitment to creative expression.

Location: 1 E Main St, Mesa, AZ 85201, USA

Closest City or Town: Paradise Valley, AZ ·

How to Get There: To get to the Mesa Arts Center in downtown Mesa, Arizona, head towards the intersection of Main Street and Center Street. Input the address 1 E Main St into your GPS or navigation app for precise directions. Whether driving, using public transportation, or taking the light rail, follow the routes that lead to Main Street, where the Mesa Arts Center is located.

GPS Coordinates: 33.4140° N, 111.8305° W

Best Time to Visit: Throughout the year.

Pass/Permit/fees: Entry is free.

Did you Know? It is known for its art activities.

6. Arizona Museum of Natural History

The Arizona Museum of Natural History in Mesa, Arizona, is a captivating destination for those intrigued by the wonders of natural history and anthropology. This premier museum showcases diverse exhibits, including dinosaur fossils, ancient Native American artifacts, and immersive displays of Arizona's geological and cultural heritage. Visitors can observe a life-size replica of a T-Rex skeleton, explore interactive exhibits, and even dig for fossils in the famous Paleo Dig Pit. With its engaging educational programs and fascinating collections, the Arizona Museum of Natural History offers an enriching and entertaining experience for all ages.

Location: 53 N Macdonald, Mesa, AZ 85201, USA

Closest City or Town: Paradise Valley, AZ ·

How to Get There: To reach the Arizona Museum of Natural History in Mesa, Arizona, head towards the intersection of Main Street and MacDonald Street.

GPS Coordinates: 33.4166° N, 111.8337° W

Best Time to Visit: Throughout the year.

Pass/Permit/fees: The ticket costs $7-$13. Kids under 2 are free.

Did you Know? It is a great place to learn different activities.

GILBERT

1. Riparian Preserve at Water Ranch

The Riparian Preserve at Water Ranch is a serene oasis in the heart of Gilbert, Arizona. This 110-acre nature preserves and wetland habitat provides a haven for diverse plant and animal species, making it a paradise for birdwatchers and nature enthusiasts. Visitors can explore the network of walking trails, observe vibrant migratory birds, and enjoy the tranquil beauty of the ponds and marshes. The preserve also offers educational programs, guided tours, and interactive exhibits, allowing visitors to learn about the importance of water conservation and the delicate balance of ecosystems.

Location: 2757 E Guadalupe Rd, Gilbert, AZ 85234, USA

Closest City or Town: Chandler, AZ · Mesa, AZ

How to Get There: To reach the Riparian Preserve at Water Ranch in Gilbert, Arizona, head towards the intersection of Greenfield Road and Guadalupe Road. Input the address 2757 E. Guadalupe Road into your GPS or navigation app for precise directions. Upon arrival, look for designated parking areas and enjoy visiting this peaceful nature preserve.

GPS Coordinates: 33.3644° N, 111.7347° W

Best Time to Visit: Throughout the year.

Pass/Permit/fees: Entry is free.

Did you Know? It offers a peaceful escape into the wonders of nature.

2. Hale Centre Theatre

The Hale Centre Theatre is a renowned theater in Gilbert, Arizona, known for its exceptional performances and immersive theatrical experiences. This state-of-the-art theater provides a unique in-the-round seating arrangement, allowing the audience to feel intimately connected to the stage. From Broadway musicals to classic plays and original productions, the Hale Centre Theatre offers various shows that captivate and entertain. With its talented cast, high production values, and commitment to excellence, the theater has earned a reputation for delivering top-quality performances.

Location: 50 W Page Ave, Gilbert, AZ 85233, USA

Closest City or Town: Chandler, AZ · Mesa, AZ

How to Get There: To reach the Hale Centre Theatre in Gilbert, Arizona, head towards the intersection of Page Avenue and Gilbert Road. Input the 50 W Page Ave address into your GPS or navigation app for precise directions.

GPS Coordinates: 33.3552° N, 111.7906° W

Best Time to Visit: Throughout the year.

Pass/Permit/fees: Different packages are available.

Did you Know? You can enjoy the captivating performances at the theater.

CHANDLER

1.   KOLI Equestrian Center

The KOLI Equestrian Center in Chandler, Arizona, offers an unforgettable horseback riding experience amidst the stunning Sonoran Desert landscape. With a focus on Native American culture, the center provides guided trail rides that allow visitors to connect with nature while learning about the region's rich history. Riders of all skill levels can explore scenic trails, spot wildlife and enjoy breathtaking views. The center also offers horsemanship lessons, special events, and even sunset rides for a truly magical experience. Whether you are looking for adventure, relaxation, or a unique cultural encounter, the KOLI Equestrian Center provides an exceptional equestrian experience that will leave a lasting impression.

Location: 6940 W BROKEN EAR RD, Chandler, AZ 85226, USA

Closest City or Town: Gilbert, AZ ·

How to Get There: To get to the KOLI Equestrian Center in Chandler, Arizona, head towards the intersection of Combs Road and Hawes Road. Input the address 2831 E. Combs Rd into your GPS or navigation app for precise directions.

GPS Coordinates: 33.2635° N, 112.0009° W

Best Time to Visit: Throughout the year.

Pass/Permit/fees: Different packages are available.

Did you Know? You can enjoy your horseback riding experience at the center.

APACHE JUNCTION

1. Lost Dutchman State Park

Lost Dutchman State Park is a beautiful desert oasis in the Superstition Mountains of Arizona, USA. Spread across 320 acres, this natural treasure offers diverse recreational activities and breathtaking scenic beauty. Named after the legendary Lost Dutchman's Gold Mine, the park attracts hikers, campers, and nature enthusiasts from far and wide. Its extensive trail system, including the famous Siphon Draw Trail, provides stunning vistas of rugged canyons, wildflowers, and towering saguaro cacti. Visitors can also explore the park's rich history at the onsite museum or enjoy picnicking, birdwatching, and stargazing.

Location: 6109 N Apache Trail, Apache Junction, AZ 85119, USA

Closest City or Town: Gilbert, AZ ·

How to Get There: Lost Dutchman State Park is near Apache Junction, Arizona, approximately 40 miles east of downtown Phoenix. Take U.S. Route 60 (Superstition Freeway) eastbound, Exit 196 for Idaho Road/AZ-88, and follow AZ-88 for about 5 miles to reach the park entrance.

GPS Coordinates: 33.4630° N, 111.4806° W

Best Time to Visit: October-April

Pass/Permit/fees: Different packages are available.

Did you Know? It is a haven for adventure and tranquillity, drawing visitors into its enchanting wilderness.

2. Goldfield Ghost Town in Apache Junction

Goldfield Ghost Town, nestled in the picturesque town of Apache Junction, Arizona, is a fascinating and well-preserved relic of the Old West. This historic attraction transports visitors back in time to the days of the Gold Rush, with its rustic buildings, dusty streets, and tales of prospectors seeking fortune. Explore the reconstructed town, complete with saloons, a mine tour, and a museum showcasing artifacts from the era. Enjoy live reenactments, gold panning, and horseback rides, immersing yourself in the spirit of the Wild West.

Location: 4650 N Mammoth Mine Rd, Apache Junction, AZ 85119, USA

Closest City or Town: Fountain Hills, AZ ·

How to Get There: Goldfield Ghost Town in Apache Junction is on the Apache Trail (AZ-88). Take Route 60 eastbound from Phoenix, then Exit 196 for Idaho Road/AZ-88. Follow AZ-88 for about 4 miles to reach Goldfield Ghost Town on your right.

GPS Coordinates: 33.4572° N, 111.4919° W

Best Time to Visit: Summer, Fall

Pass/Permit/fees: Different packages are available.

Did you Know? It is a captivating destination that captures the essence of Arizona's rich mining history.

3.   Superstition Mountains

The Superstition Mountains in central Arizona stand as an awe-inspiring and rugged range of peaks. These majestic mountains hold a rich history steeped in folklore and legends. Known for their striking beauty, the Superstitions offer breathtaking panoramic views, towering cliffs, deep canyons, and unique rock formations. It is a heaven for outdoor enthusiasts, with numerous hiking trails, including the famous Peralta Trail, leading adventurers to hidden treasures and scenic vistas. From the mysterious lure of the Lost Dutchman's Gold Mine to the diverse desert flora and fauna, the Superstition Mountains capture the imagination and offer a remarkable wilderness experience.

Location: Arizona 85119, USA

Closest City or Town: Fountain Hills, AZ ·

How to Get There: To reach the Superstition Mountains in Arizona, take State Route 88 (Apache Trail) from Apache Junction. Access points include the Peralta Trailhead and Lost Dutchman State Park, both off Apache Trail.

GPS Coordinates: 33.4755° N, 111.1937° W

Best Time to Visit: Summer, Fall

Pass/Permit/fees: Entry is free.

Did you Know? It is an ideal place for mountain lovers.

4.   Superstition Mountain Museum

The Superstition Mountain Museum in Apache Junction, Arizona, is a captivating destination that encapsulates the legendary Superstition Mountains' rich history and folklore. Spanning 12 acres, this remarkable museum offers visitors a glimpse into the region's vibrant past. Showcasing an extensive collection of artifacts, photographs, and exhibits, the museum beautifully narrates the tales of the Lost Dutchman's Gold Mine and the enigmatic characters who ventured into the treacherous mountains in search of untold riches. With its picturesque surroundings and engaging displays, the Superstition Mountain Museum serves as a gateway to the past.

Location: 4087 E Apache Trail, Apache Junction, AZ 85119, USA

Closest City or Town: Fountain Hills, AZ ·

How to Get There: Visitors can reach the museum by car, following US-60 East to Apache Junction and then turning onto Highway 88. Public transportation options are also available, with bus services to Apache Junction and then using a taxi or rideshare to reach the museum.

GPS Coordinates: 33.4471° N, 111.5017° W

Best Time to Visit: Throughout the year.

Pass/Permit/fees: The ticket costs $11-$23.

Did you Know? It is famous for its heritage and the allure of the Superstition Mountains.

TORTILLA FLAT

1. Canyon Lake

Canyon Lake, located in the magnificent Superstition Mountains of Arizona, is a stunning reservoir renowned for its natural beauty and recreational opportunities. Surrounded by rugged cliffs and desert landscapes, the lake offers a picturesque setting for boating, fishing, and water sports. With over 28 miles of shoreline, visitors can explore secluded coves, swim in crystal-clear waters, or relax on sandy beaches. Scenic boat tours and kayak rentals allow an up-close encounter with the lake's striking rock formations and diverse wildlife. Canyon Lake is a captivating destination that invites outdoor enthusiasts to immerse themselves in its tranquil and breathtaking surroundings.

Location: Canyon Lake, Arizona, USA

Closest City or Town: Apache Junction, AZ

How to Get There: To reach Canyon Lake in Arizona, take State Route 88 (Apache Trail) from Apache Junction. Follow Apache Trail for approximately 15 miles until you reach the turnoff for Canyon Lake Marina.

GPS Coordinates: 33.5422° N, 111.4365° W

Best Time to Visit: Summer, Fall

Pass/Permit/fees: Different packages are available for reservation.

Did you Know? It is famous for its beautiful views.

COOLIDGE

1. Casa Grande Ruins National Monument

Casa Grande Ruins National Monument, located in Coolidge, Arizona, is a mesmerizing archaeological site preserving the remnants of an ancient Sonoran Desert farming community. The park's centerpiece is the Casa Grande ("Great House"), a four-story adobe structure believed to have been built by the Hohokam people around 1350 AD. Visitors can explore the ruins, marvel at the impressive architectural design, and learn about Hohokam's advanced irrigation systems. The on-site museum offers exhibits showcasing artifacts and providing insights into the culture and history of the Hohokam civilization.

Location: 1100 W Ruins Dr, Coolidge, AZ 85128, USA

Closest City or Town: Florence, AZ ·

How to Get There: To get to Casa Grande Ruins National Monument in Coolidge, Arizona, take Interstate 10 and exit at 194 for Florence Boulevard (State Route 287)—Head east on Florence Boulevard for about 9 miles until you reach the park entrance on the right.

GPS Coordinates: 32.9974° N, 111.5325° W

Best Time to Visit: Throughout the year

Pass/Permit/fees: Different packages are available.

Did you Know? It offers a captivating journey back in time to a fascinating chapter of Native American history.

PICACHO

1.   Rooster Cogburn Ostrich Ranch

The Rooster Cogburn Ostrich Ranch is a unique and fascinating attraction in Picacho, Arizona. This ranch offers visitors the opportunity to interact with a variety of exotic animals, with ostriches being the main highlight. The farm is named after the iconic character "Rooster Cogburn" from the movie "True Grit", played by John Wayne. At the ranch, visitors can feed and pet these magnificent creatures, take guided tours to learn about their habits and biology, and even have the opportunity to ride an ostrich. In addition to the ostriches, the ranch also houses other animals like miniature donkeys, deer, turtles, and goats, providing a delightful experience for animal lovers of all ages.

Location: 17599 E Peak Ln, Picacho, AZ 85141, USA

Closest City or Town: Eloy, AZ

How to Get There: It is easily accessible from Interstate 10. Exit 219 onto Picacho Peak Road and follow the signs to the 17599 E Peak Lane ranch. Enjoy a memorable experience with exotic animals, including ostriches, miniature donkeys, and more.

GPS Coordinates: 32.6879° N , 111.4816° W

Best Time to Visit: April-November

Pass/Permit/fees: The ticket costs $12-$15.

Did you Know? It is famous for its scenic surroundings and special activities.

2.   Picacho Peak State Park

Picacho Peak State Park in Arizona is a natural treasure offering breathtaking scenery and outdoor adventures. This iconic park is dominated by the prominent Picacho Peak, a volcanic mountain over 1,500 feet. Visitors can embark on exhilarating hikes along various trails, including the challenging Hunter Trail that leads to the summit, rewarding hikers with panoramic views of the surrounding Sonoran Desert. The park is also a haven for wildlife enthusiasts, with bird-watching opportunities and spotting desert wildlife. Picacho Peak State Park provides a perfect blend of nature, recreation, and exploration, making it a must-visit destination for outdoor enthusiasts and nature lovers.

Location: Pinal, Arizona, United States

Closest City or Town: Coolidge, AZ ·

How to Get There: To reach Picacho Peak State Park in Arizona, take Exit 219 from Interstate 10 and head south on Picacho Peak Road. Follow the signs to the park's entrance at 15520 Picacho Peak Road.

GPS Coordinates: 32.6351° N, 111.4007° W

Best Time to Visit: Spring, Fall

Pass/Permit/fees: Online reservations are available.

Did you Know? It is heaven for wildlife and bird lovers.

WICKENBURG

1. Desert Caballeros Western Museum

The Desert Caballeros Western Museum, located in Wickenburg, Arizona, is a cultural gem that celebrates the rich history and heritage of the American West. This museum showcases an extensive collection of Western art, artifacts, and exhibits that beautifully depict the spirit of the frontier. Visitors can explore stunning displays featuring cowboy culture, Native American art, mining history, and the stories of the pioneers who shaped the region. The museum offers educational programs, special events, and art exhibitions, providing a dynamic and immersive experience for all ages.

Location: 21 N Frontier St, Wickenburg, AZ 85390, USA

Closest City or Town: Sun City West, AZ ·

How to Get There: To reach the Desert Caballeros Western Museum in Wickenburg, Arizona, take US-60 (W. Wickenburg Way) towards downtown Wickenburg. Turn right onto N. Tegner Street, and you will find the museum at 21 N. Frontier Street.

GPS Coordinates: 33.9686° N, 112.7311° W

Best Time to Visit: Summer, Fall

Pass/Permit/fees: Different packages are available.

Did you Know? You can enjoy and explore the rich Western heritage showcased within its walls.

SUPERIOR

1. Boyce Thompson Arboretum

Boyce Thompson Arboretum, located in Superior, Arizona, is a botanical paradise that delights nature enthusiasts and plant lovers alike. Spanning over 300 acres, this living museum showcases a diverse collection of desert plants worldwide. Visitors can wander through winding paths, surrounded by vibrant gardens, towering cacti, and lush trees. The nursery also offers educational programs, guided tours, and seasonal events that provide insight into the fascinating world of plants and their ecological importance. With its stunning landscapes, tranquil atmosphere, and wealth of botanical wonders, Boyce Thompson Arboretum offers a captivating experience and a chance to connect with nature's beauty.

Location: 37615 E Arboretum Way, Superior, AZ 85173, USA

Closest City or Town: Floernce, AZ ·

How to Get There: To reach Boyce Thompson Arboretum in Superior, Arizona, take US-60 (E. US Highway 60) towards Superior. Follow the signs directing you to the arboretum, located at 37615 E. US Highway 60.

GPS Coordinates: 33.2787° N, 111.1592° W

Best Time to Visit: March-May

Pass/Permit/fees: The ticket costs $3-$20.

Did you Know? You can enjoy a peaceful and educational experience surrounded by stunning desert landscapes and various plants.

TUCSON

1. Gates Pass

Gates Pass is a mesmerizing natural wonder that captivates visitors with its stunning panoramic views and rugged desert landscapes. Nestled in the Tucson Mountains, this scenic mountain pass offers a gateway to breathtaking vistas of the surrounding Sonoran Desert. As the sun sets over the horizon, the access transforms into a magical spectacle, with vibrant hues of orange and purple painting the sky. Hikers and nature enthusiasts flock to Gates Pass to explore its trails, soak in the serene ambiance, and marvel at the diverse flora and fauna that thrive in this arid region. A visit to Gates Pass is an unforgettable journey into the heart of Arizona's natural beauty.

Location: 6400 W Gates Pass Rd Tucson, AZ 85745

Closest City or Town: Flowing Wells, AZ

How to Get There: Head west on West Speedway Boulevard from downtown Tucson to reach Gates Pass in Arizona. Turn left onto North Camino de Oeste and follow through the Tucson Mountains until you reach Gates Pass.

GPS Coordinates: 32.2223° N, 111.1009° W

Best Time to Visit: Summer, Spring

Pass/Permit/fees: Different packages are available.

Did you Know? Visitors can explore the trails and viewpoints for stunning views of the Sonoran Desert.

2. Catalina State Park

Catalina State Park in the north of Tucson, Arizona, is a breathtaking desert oasis offering many outdoor adventures. Spanning over 5,500 acres at the base of the majestic Santa Catalina Mountains, the park boasts diverse landscapes, from desert valleys to lush riparian areas. Hiking trails weave through the picturesque scenery, showcasing stunning vistas and opportunities for wildlife sightings. The park also features picnic areas, campgrounds, and equestrian facilities, catering to various outdoor enthusiasts. With its tranquil ambiance, Catalina State Park is a haven for nature lovers, providing a perfect escape from bustling city life.

Location: 11570 N Oracle Rd, Tucson, AZ 85737, USA

Closest City or Town: Catalina Foothills, AZ

How to Get There: To reach Catalina State Park, drive north on Oracle Road (Highway 77) from Tucson for approximately 16 miles. Look for the park entrance on the right-hand side. Public transportation options are limited, but you can consider taking a bus or taxi to a nearby area and arranging a rideshare service or shuttle to take you to the park. Bicycling or walking along Oracle Road is also an option if you are in the vicinity.

GPS Coordinates: 32.4364° N, 110.9096° W

Best Time to Visit: October- April

Pass/Permit/fees: The ticket costs $7-$30.

Did you Know? It is an ideal place for nature lovers.

3. Arizona-Sonora Desert Museum

The Arizona-Sonora Desert Museum, nestled in the stunning Sonoran Desert near Tucson, Arizona, is a captivating blend of a zoo, botanical garden, and natural history museum. Spread over 98 acres, the museum showcases the unique flora and fauna of the region, offering visitors an immersive experience. From towering saguaro cacti to elusive desert animals, the museum's exhibits and interactive displays provide a glimpse into the intricate ecosystems of the desert. Visitors can explore winding desert trails, attend live animal presentations, and marvel at the diverse plant life.

Location: 2021 N Kinney Rd, Tucson, AZ 85743, USA

Closest City or Town: Drexel Heights, AZ

How to Get There: To get to the Arizona-Sonora Desert Museum near Tucson, Arizona, drive west on West Speedway Boulevard (State Route 77) and turn left onto Kinney Road. Continue for about 2 miles until you reach the museum entrance on your right. Public transportation is limited, so consider taking a bus to the Tucson Transit Center downtown and then using a taxi or rideshare service to reach the museum. Tour companies also offer

guided trips to the museum, providing transportation as part of their itinerary.

GPS Coordinates: 32.2440° N, 111.1682° W

Best Time to Visit: October- April

Pass/Permit/fees: The ticket costs $20-$28. Kids under 3 are free.

Did you Know? It is famous for the beauty and fragility of desert environments.

4. The Gaslight Theatre

The Gaslight Theatre in Tucson, Arizona, is a delightful entertainment venue that transports visitors to a bygone era of melodrama, laughter, and musical performances. With its old-fashioned charm and vaudevillian-style shows, the Gaslight Theatre offers an immersive experience for all ages. Audiences can enjoy live musical productions filled with catchy tunes, hilarious comedy skits, and interactive performances that encourage participation. The theater's talented cast and crew bring the stage to life, creating a lively atmosphere that leaves guests smiling and tapping their feet. Whether it is a family outing, a date night, or a gathering of friends, the Gaslight Theatre promises lively entertainment and nostalgic fun.

Location: 7010 E Broadway Blvd, Tucson, AZ 85710, USA

Closest City or Town: Drexel Heights, AZ

How to Get There: To get to The Gaslight Theatre in Tucson, Arizona, drive east on East Broadway Boulevard until you reach the intersection with South Kolb Road. The theater will be on your left-hand side. Public transportation options are limited, but you can consider taking a bus to a nearby area and then using a taxi or rideshare service to reach the theater.

GPS Coordinates: 32.2203° N, 110.8433° W

Best Time to Visit: Throughout the year.

Pass/Permit/fees: The ticket costs $20.

Did you Know? It is a perfect place for entertainment and fun.

5. The Mini Time Machine Museum of Miniatures

The Mini Time Machine Museum of Miniatures, located in Tucson, Arizona, is a whimsical and enchanting destination that celebrates the artistry and craftsmanship of miniature creations. This extraordinary museum showcases an extensive collection of meticulously crafted miniatures spanning different eras and themes. The museum offers a fascinating journey through representations, from intricately detailed dollhouses to tiny furniture, artwork, and even tiny mechanical wonders. Visitors of all age groups can marvel at the remarkable attention to detail and immerse themselves in the magical world of models. The Mini Time Machine Museum is a testament to the beauty of small-scale creations and a delightful experience for all who visit.

Location: 4455 E Camp Lowell Dr, Tucson, AZ 85712, USA

Closest City or Town: Casas Adobes, AZ

How to Get There: To get to The Mini Time Machine Museum of Miniatures in Tucson, Arizona, drive north on North Campbell Avenue from downtown until you reach East Pima Street. Turn right onto East Pima Street, and the museum will be on your left at the intersection of East Pima Street and North Edith Boulevard. Public transportation options are limited, so consider taking a bus to a nearby area and then using a taxi or rideshare service to reach the museum.

GPS Coordinates: 32.2505° N, 110.9031° W

Best Time to Visit: Throughout the year.

Pass/Permit/fees: The ticket costs $8-$12.

Did you Know? It is a home of miniature creations.

6. DeGrazia Gallery in the Sun Museum

The DeGrazia Gallery in the Sun Museum in Tucson, Arizona, is a vibrant and captivating art destination celebrating the colorful works of renowned artist Ettore "Ted" DeGrazia. The museum showcases DeGrazia's diverse collection of paintings, ceramics, sculptures, and jewelry amidst the stunning Sonoran Desert landscape. Visitors can explore the charming adobe buildings, wander through outdoor courtyards adorned with murals, and discover the unique artistic vision of DeGrazia. The museum also hosts rotating exhibits, cultural events, and workshops, offering a dynamic and immersive experience for art enthusiasts and curious minds alike.

Location: 6300 N Swan Rd, Tucson, AZ 85718, USA

Closest City or Town: OroValley, AZ.

How to Get There: To get to the DeGrazia Gallery in the Sun Museum in Tucson, Arizona, drive north on North Swan Road until you reach the intersection with East Prince Road. The museum will be on your left-hand side. Public transportation options are limited, so consider taking a bus to a nearby area and then using a taxi or rideshare service to reach the museum.

GPS Coordinates: 32.2948° N, 110.9242° W

Best Time to Visit: Throughout the year.

Pass/Permit/fees: The ticket costs $5-$8. Kids under 12 are free.

Did you Know? It is an artistic legacy and a delightful celebration of Southwest art.

7. University of Arizona

The University of Arizona, located in Tucson, is a prestigious institution known for its excellence in education, research, and innovation. With a history of over a century, the university offers a wide range of academic programs across various disciplines. From engineering and business to the arts and sciences, students can pursue their passions and receive a quality education. The campus boasts state-of-the-art facilities, vibrant student life, and a supportive community. The University of Arizona is a hub of intellectual growth and cultural diversity, shaping the minds of future leaders and making significant contributions to society.

Location: Tucson, AZ 85721, USA

Closest City or Town: ·Marana, AZ

How to Get There: To get to the University of Arizona in Tucson, Arizona, take East Broadway Boulevard westbound until you reach North Euclid Avenue. The university will be on your left-hand side. Public transportation options include taking the Sun Link streetcar or utilizing nearby bus routes.

GPS Coordinates: 32.2319° N, 110.9501° W

Best Time to Visit: Throughout the year.

Pass/Permit/fees: Entry is free.

Did you Know? It is a famous learning place.

8. Madera Canyon

Madera Canyon, located in the Santa Rita Mountains of southern Arizona, is a nature lover's paradise. This picturesque canyon is known for its stunning beauty and diverse wildlife, making it a popular destination for outdoor enthusiasts and birdwatchers. The canyon is home to over 250 species of birds, including elegant hummingbirds and colorful painted buntings. Hiking trails wind through lush pine and oak forests, offering breathtaking views of the surrounding peaks and valleys. Visitors can also enjoy camping, picnicking, and horseback riding in this tranquil oasis. Madera Canyon is a true gem, captivating visitors with its natural splendor and peaceful ambiance.

Location: Santa Rita Mountains, Arizona, US

Closest City or Town: Green Valley, AZ.

How to Get There: From Tucson, take I-19 south to Exit 63 for Green Valley/Madera Canyon. Follow White House Canyon Road for 13 miles to reach the picturesque Madera Canyon.

GPS Coordinates: 31.7251° N, 110.8801° W

Best Time to Visit: Summer, Spring.

Pass/Permit/fees: The ticket costs $5.

Did you Know? It is a home of natural and quiet beauty.

9. Red Hills Visitor Center

The Red Hills Visitor Center, situated in the heart of the Saguaro National Park in Tucson, Arizona, is a gateway to the enchanting desert landscape. This educational hub offers a wealth of information on the park's unique ecosystem and cultural history. Visitors can explore interactive exhibits, learn about desert wildlife and plant adaptations, and even participate in ranger-led programs and guided hikes. The center also features a gift shop where one can find books, souvenirs, and artwork showcasing the Sonoran Desert's beauty. With its informative displays and immersive experiences, the Red Hills Visitor Center is an ideal starting point for discovering the wonders of Saguaro National Park.

Location: 2700 N Kinney Rd, Tucson, AZ 85743, USA

Closest City or Town: Flowing Wells,

How to Get There: From Tucson, head east on Speedway Boulevard or Broadway Boulevard to enter Saguaro National Park East. Follow the signs for approximately 8 miles to reach the Red Hills Visitor Center.

GPS Coordinates: 32.2544° N, 111.1973° W

Best Time to Visit: Summer, fall.

Pass/Permit/fees: The ticket costs $15.

Did you Know? It is famous for a wide range of activities.

10. Pima Air and Space Museum

The Pima Air and Space Museum in Tucson, Arizona, is a captivating destination for aviation enthusiasts and history buffs. With its vast collection of over 350 aircraft spread across 80 acres, the museum offers a glimpse into the fantastic world of flight. Visitors can explore aircraft ranging from vintage biplanes to modern military jets, including iconic models like the B-29 Superfortress and the SR-71 Blackbird. The museum also houses exhibits showcasing the evolution of space exploration, with artifacts from NASA's missions. With knowledgeable staff, engaging displays, and firsthand opportunities to witness restoration efforts, the Pima Air and Space Museum provides an immersive and educational experience for all ages.

Location: 6000 E Valencia Rd, Tucson, AZ 85756, USA

Closest City or Town: Drexel Heights, AZ

How to Get There: Pima Air and Space Museum in Tucson, Arizona, can be reached by car (6000 E Valencia Rd) or public transportation (Sun Tran).

GPS Coordinates: 32.1390° N, 110.8687° W

Best Time to Visit: Throughout the year.

Pass/Permit/fees: The ticket costs $13-$26.

Did you Know? It is a famous place to learn about aircraft.

11. Sabino Canyon

Sabino Canyon, nestled in the Santa Catalina Mountains near Tucson, Arizona, is a natural wonderland that beckons outdoor enthusiasts. This stunning desert oasis offers a variety of activities for visitors to enjoy. Hiking trails wind through picturesque landscapes, showcasing the region's unique flora and fauna. The Sabino Creek meanders through the canyon, offering refreshing opportunities for swimming and picnicking. For a more leisurely experience, the Sabino Canyon Tram Tour offers a narrated journey through the breathtaking scenery. Whether you are looking for adventure or tranquility, Sabino Canyon offers a captivating escape into nature's beauty, making it a must-visit destination for nature lovers.

Location: 5700 N Sabino Canyon Rd, Tucson, AZ 85750, United States

Closest City or Town: Casas Adobes, AZ · Oro Valley, AZ · Marana, AZ · Green Valley, AZ

How to Get There: To reach Sabino Canyon in Tucson, Arizona, drive to 5700 N Sabino Canyon Rd or take a Sun Tran bus.

GPS Coordinates: 32.3224° N, 110.8099° W

Best Time to Visit: Spring, Summer.

Pass/Permit/fees: The day pass costs $13-$26.

Did you Know? It is a treat to watch for nature lovers.

12.   Mission San Xavier del Bac

Mission San Xavier del Bac, located just outside Tucson, Arizona, is a beautiful testament to the region's rich history and cultural heritage. This Spanish colonial mission, founded in 1692, showcases stunning Baroque architecture and intricate artwork. The ornate interior features vibrant frescoes, wooden carvings, and decorative details that blend European and Native American influences. Visitors can explore the mission's museum, attend religious services, or simply admire the beauty of the surrounding desert landscape. Mission San Xavier del Bac is a pilgrimage site for both spiritual and historical significance, offering a glimpse into the enduring legacy of early Spanish colonization in the American Southwest.

Location: 1950 W San Xavier Rd, Tucson, AZ 85746, USA

Closest City or Town: Oro Valley, AZ

How to Get There: To reach Mission San Xavier del Bac, drive to 1950 W San Xavier Rd, Tucson, AZ 85746, or take a Sun Tran bus. Rideshare services like Uber and Lyft are also available.

GPS Coordinates: 32.1070° N, 111.0088° W

Best Time to Visit: Throughout the year.

Pass/Permit/fees: Entry is free.

Did you Know? It is famous for its spiritual and historical value.

13.   Tohono Chul

Tohono Chul, located in Tucson, Arizona, is a tranquil desert oasis that celebrates the beauty of nature and culture. This botanical garden and nature offer visitors a captivating experience amidst its diverse flora and fauna. Wander through enchanting gardens filled with native plants, explore winding trails that showcase the Sonoran Desert's unique ecosystem, and admire stunning art installations that reflect the region's rich heritage. The Tohono Chul Galleries features rotating exhibits showcasing local and international artists. With its peaceful ambiance, educational programs, and delightful gift shop, Tohono Chul provides a serene escape and an appreciation for the wonders of the desert landscape.

Location: 7366 N Paseo Del Norte, Tucson, AZ 85704, USA

Closest City or Town: Marana, AZ

How to Get There: To reach Tohono Chul in Tucson, Arizona, drive to 7366 N Paseo del Norte or take a Sun Tran bus.

GPS Coordinates: 32.3395° N, 110.9817° W

Best Time to Visit: October- April.

Pass/Permit/fees: The ticket costs $4.

Did you Know? It is famous for its desert landscape view.

14.   Saguaro National Park

Saguaro National Park in southern Arizona is a breathtaking sanctuary celebrating the majestic saguaro cactus and the vibrant desert landscape. The Rincon Mountain District boasts scenic drives, hiking trails, and panoramic views from high elevations. The Tucson Mountain District showcases a desert oasis with picturesque trails and impressive saguaro forests. Visitors can marvel at the towering cacti, explore ancient petroglyphs, and witness stunning sunsets that paint the sky.

With its unique ecosystem, rich biodiversity, and opportunities for outdoor recreation, Saguaro National Park is a captivating destination for nature lovers and adventure seekers alike.

Location: Arizona, USA

Closest City or Town: Green Valley, AZ

How to Get There: To reach Saguaro National Park in Arizona, drive to either the Rincon Mountain District (3693 S Old Spanish Trail, Tucson, AZ 85730) or the Tucson Mountain District (2700 N Kinney Road, Tucson, AZ 85743). Use GPS or online maps for specific directions.

GPS Coordinates: 32.2967° N, 111.1666° W

Best Time to Visit: Throughout the year.

Pass/Permit/fees: The ticket costs $15.

Did you Know? The park offers diverse experiences.

15. Rincon Mountain Visitor Center

The Rincon Mountain Visitor Center is a welcoming gateway to the natural wonders of Saguaro National Park's Rincon Mountain District. Located in Tucson, Arizona, this center serves as an information hub for visitors. You will find exhibits that provide insights into the park's diverse ecosystems, wildlife, and cultural history. Knowledgeable park rangers are on hand to answer questions and offer guidance on trails, scenic drives, and points of interest. The center also offers maps, books, and educational materials to enhance exploration. Whether you are a first-time visitor or a seasoned explorer, the Rincon Mountain Visitor Center is an invaluable resource for making the most of your Saguaro National Park experience.

Location: 3693 S Old Spanish Trail, Tucson, AZ 85730, USA

Closest City or Town: Flowing Wells, AZ

How to Get There: To get to the Rincon Mountain Visitor Center in Saguaro National Park's Rincon Mountain District:

1. Drive to Tucson, Arizona.

2. Take East Broadway Boulevard from Tucson until it becomes S Old Spanish Trail.

3. Follow the signs to Saguaro National Park East.

GPS Coordinates: 32.1802° N, 110.7363° W

Best Time to Visit: Throughout the year.

Pass/Permit/fees: Entry is free.

Did you Know? It is famous for its wildlife.

16. Reid Park Zoo

Reid Park Zoo, located in Tucson, Arizona, is a vibrant and engaging destination for wildlife enthusiasts of all ages. This zoological park showcases a diverse array of animals from around the world. Visitors can witness beautiful animal encounters, explore immersive exhibits, and participate in educational programs that promote conservation and environmental awareness. From the playful antics of meerkats to the majestic presence of lions, the zoo offers a close-up experience with various species. With beautiful landscaping, interactive displays, and a commitment to animal welfare, Reid Park Zoo provides visitors with a memorable and enriching experience while fostering a deeper understanding and appreciation of the natural world.

Location: 3400 E Zoo Ct, Tucson, AZ 85716, USA

Closest City or Town: Green Valley, AZ

How to Get There: To reach Reid Park Zoo in Tucson, Arizona, drive to 3400 E Zoo Ct or take a Sun Tran bus. Rideshare services like Uber and Lyft are also available.

GPS Coordinates: 32.2099° N, 110.9207° W

Best Time to Visit: October- April.

Pass/Permit/fees: The ticket costs $7-$11. Kids under 1 are free.

Did you Know? It is an ideal place for wildlife lovers.

17. Tucson Botanical Gardens

Tucson Botanical Gardens, nestled in the heart of Tucson, Arizona, is a serene oasis that celebrates the beauty and diversity of desert flora. Spread across 5.5 acres, the gardens offer a delightful escape into nature's tranquility. Visitors can wander through themed gardens showcasing various plants, including cacti, succulents, and vibrant seasonal blooms. The enchanting Butterfly and Hummingbird Gardens attract a variety of colorful winged visitors. With educational exhibits, art installations, and peaceful pathways, Tucson Botanical Gardens provides a captivating experience for nature enthusiasts, garden lovers, and those seeking a quiet retreat amid the desert landscape.

Location: 2150 N Alvernon Way, Tucson, AZ 85712, USA

Closest City or Town: Green Valley, AZ

How to Get There: To reach Tucson Botanical Gardens in Tucson, Arizona, drive to 2150 N Alvernon Way or take a Sun Tran bus.

GPS Coordinates: 32.2485° N, 110.9088° W

Best Time to Visit: October- April.

Pass/Permit/fees: The ticket costs $8-$15. Kids under 4 are free.

Did you Know? It is famous for its beauty and various events.

MOUNT LEMMON

1. Mount Lemmon

Mount Lemmon, located in the Santa Catalina Mountains near Tucson, Arizona, is a breathtaking destination that offers a refreshing escape from the desert heat. This majestic mountain is a haven for outdoor enthusiasts and nature lovers. Adventurers can enjoy scenic hikes and mountain biking or enjoy a picturesque drive along the winding Catalina Highway. The mountain's diverse ecosystems support a wide variety of wildlife, and its cool, alpine climate provides respite during the hot summer months, with stunning vistas, pine forests, and opportunities for outdoor recreation.

Location: Tucson, Pima County, Arizona, U.S.

Closest City or Town: Scottsdale, AZ.

How to Get There: To reach Mount Lemmon in Arizona, drive to Tucson and take the Catalina Highway (Mount Lemmon Highway). The highway starts at the junction of East Tanque Verde Road and North Houghton Road. Check local road conditions and weather forecasts before your trip.

GPS Coordinates: 32.4434° N, 110.7881° W

Best Time to Visit: October-November.

Pass/Permit/fees: Entry is free.

Did you Know? It is a captivating destination for all to enjoy.

2. Mt. Lemmon SkyCenter Observatory

The Mt. Lemmon SkyCenter Observatory, located atop the picturesque Mt. Lemmon in Arizona, is a haven for astronomy enthusiasts and stargazers alike. Perched at 9,157 feet, it offers a unique and pristine environment for observing the night sky. Equipped with state-of-the-art telescopes, the observatory provides breathtaking views of distant galaxies, nebulae, and celestial objects. The knowledgeable staff and astronomers at the SkyCenter offer engaging and informative guided tours, taking visitors on a journey through the wonders of the universe. Whether exploring the cosmos, attending educational programs, or participating in nighttime observing sessions.

Location: 9800 E Ski Run Rd, Mt Lemmon, AZ 85619, USA

Closest City or Town: Mesa, AZ.

How to Get There: Drive along the Catalina Highway from Tucson to reach the Mt. Lemmon SkyCenter Observatory in Arizona. Look for signs indicating the observatory near the summit of Mt. Lemmon. Make reservations in advance for tours and programs, and prepare for cooler temperatures at the higher elevation.

GPS Coordinates: 32.4410° N, 110.7888° W

Best Time to Visit: Spring

Pass/Permit/fees: Different packages are available.

Did you Know? It will be an unforgettable and enlightening astronomical experience.

VAIL

1. Colossal Cave Mountain Park

Nestled in the stunning Rincon Mountains of Arizona, Colossal Cave Mountain Park is a natural treasure waiting to explore. This expansive park boasts the incredible Colossal Cave, an underground wonder filled with awe-inspiring formations that have evolved for millions of years. Visitors can embark on guided tours, delving deep into the cave's mysterious passages while learning about its geological and historical significance. Above ground, the park offers scenic trails, picnic areas, horseback riding, and camping opportunities. With its rich natural beauty and captivating cave system, Colossal Cave Mountain Park provides an unforgettable adventure for nature enthusiasts and curious explorers.

Location: 16721 E Old Spanish Trail, Vail, AZ 85641, USA

Closest City or Town: Colorado, AZ.

How to Get There: To get to Colossal Cave Mountain Park in Arizona, drive southeast from Tucson on I-10 until Exit 279 for Colossal Cave Road. Follow Colossal Cave Road south for about 7 miles to get to the park entrance.

GPS Coordinates: 32.06508° N, 110.630914° W

Best Time to Visit: Spring, Summer

Pass/Permit/fees: The ticket costs $9-$18. Kids under 12 are free.

Did you Know? It is famous for its beauty and outdoor activities.

SAHUARITA

1.   Titan Missile Museum

Located in Sahuarita, Arizona, the Titan Missile Museum is a testament to the Cold War era and offers a captivating glimpse into the history of nuclear deterrence. Housed within an actual intercontinental ballistic missile (ICBM) silo, this museum provides a unique and immersive experience. Visitors can explore the underground facility, view the massive Titan II missile up close, and learn about its role in the United States' nuclear defense strategy. Engaging guided tours led by knowledgeable docents reveal fascinating insights into the technology, operations, and global tensions of the time. The Titan Missile Museum offers a thought-provoking journey into the complexities of the Cold War era and its impact on the world.

Location: 1580 W Duval Mine Rd, Green Valley, AZ 85614, USA

Closest City or Town: Green Valley, AZ.

How to Get There: To get to the Titan Missile Museum in Sahuarita, Arizona, travel south on Interstate 19 from Tucson. Take Exit 69 for Duval Mine Road and turn left. Continue on Duval Mine Road until you reach the museum's entrance at 1580 W. Duval Mine Road.

GPS Coordinates: 31.9027° N, 110.9993° W

Best Time to Visit: Spring, Summer

Pass/Permit/fees: The ticket costs $12-$16.

Did you Know? It is famous for its unique Cold War relic.

BENSON

1. Double R Ranch

Double R Ranch in Benson, Arizona, is a charming, picturesque ranch in the desert's heart. With sprawling landscapes and breathtaking views, it offers a unique Western experience. The farm is known for its dedication to raising and caring for livestock, particularly cattle. The Double R Ranch in Benson follows sustainable ranching practices, ensuring the welfare of their animals and preserving the natural beauty of the surrounding environment. Visitors to the ranch can enjoy authentic cowboy experiences, including horseback riding, cattle drives, and rustic accommodations. Double R Ranch in Benson embodies the Western spirit, offering a memorable and immersive ranching experience in Arizona's scenic desert.

Location: 440 W Cimmaron Ln, Benson, AZ 85602, USA

Closest City or Town: Tucson, AZ.

How to Get There: Double R Ranch in Benson, Arizona, can be reached by following I-10 to Benson and navigating to 440 W Cimmaron Ln, Benson, AZ, 85602. Drive safely and check for road closures or construction updates before your journey

GPS Coordinates: 32.1185° N, 110.3072° W

Best Time to Visit: Spring, Summer

Pass/Permit/fees: Different packages are available.

Did you Know? It is famous for its scenic desert landscapes.

2. Kartchner Caverns State Park

Kartchner Caverns State Park, located in Arizona, is a mesmerizing underground wonder that leaves visitors in awe. This geological gem showcases intricate limestone formations and stunning cavernous rooms, meticulously preserved to maintain their natural splendor. Guided tours take visitors through the caverns, revealing stunning stalactites, stalagmites, and delicate formations that have taken thousands of years to develop. The park also offers hiking trails, picnic areas, and educational exhibits, providing a comprehensive experience for nature enthusiasts. Kartchner Caverns State Park stands as a testament to the importance of conservation, allowing visitors to marvel at the beauty hidden beneath the surface of the Arizona desert.

Location: 2980 AZ-90, Benson, AZ 85602, USA

Closest City or Town: Green Valley, AZ.

How to Get There: To get to Kartchner Caverns State Park in Benson, Arizona, follow AZ-90 to the park's address at 2980 AZ-90. Use GPS or online maps for precise navigation, and be mindful of road closures or construction.

GPS Coordinates: 31.8366° N, 110.3489° W

Best Time to Visit: Summer, Spring

Pass/Permit/fees: The ticket costs $5-$23.

Did you Know? It is a captivating experience to explore the magnificent underground formations of Kartchner Caverns State Park.

TOMBSTONE

1. Tombstone Courthouse State Historic Park

Tombstone Courthouse State Historical Park is a captivating destination that immerses visitors in the rich history of the Wild West. Located in Tombstone, Arizona, this park preserves and showcases the original Cochise County Courthouse, built in 1882, and transports visitors back in time to the days of the famous gunfight at the O.K. Corral and the legendary figures of the Old West, such as Wyatt Earp and Doc Holliday. Exhibits and displays narrate the tales of law enforcement officers, outlaws, and the mining boom that defined this era. With its well-preserved artifacts and informative guided tours, Tombstone Courthouse State Historic Park provides a remarkable glimpse into Arizona's past.

Location: 223 E Toughnut St, Tombstone, AZ 85638, USA

Closest City or Town: Sierra Vista, AZ

How to Get There: To reach Tombstone Courthouse State, Historical Park:

1. Travel to Tombstone, Arizona, and locate the park in the town center.

2. Consider driving or using public transportation to reach the destination.

3. Follow signs and directions, and check the park's operating hours for a convenient visit.

GPS Coordinates: 31.7123° N, 110.0689° W

Best Time to Visit: March-May

Pass/Permit/fees: Entry is free.

Did you Know? You can learn about the history of Arizona.

2. O.K. Corral

The O.K. Corral is an iconic symbol of the Wild West and the legendary gunfight in Tombstone, Arizona. In 1881, this historic location became the site of a fateful shootout between lawmen, led by Wyatt Earp, and a group of outlaws, including the notorious Clanton and McLaury brothers. The gunfight lasted only about 30 seconds but left a lasting imprint on American folklore. Today, the O.K. Corral is a popular tourist attraction, offering reenactments, exhibits, and guided tours that allow visitors to step into the shoes of those involved in one of the West's most infamous events.

Location: 326 E Allen St, Tombstone, AZ 85638, USA

Closest City or Town: Naco, Mexico ·Douglas, AZ

How to Get There: To get to the O.K. Corral, travel to Tombstone, Arizona, and locate the iconic site in the town center. Choose your mode of transportation, whether it is driving, taking public transportation, or arranging for a taxi or shuttle service.

GPS Coordinates: 31.7130° N, 110.0676° W

Best Time to Visit: March-May

Pass/Permit/fees: The ticket costs $10.

Did you Know? Visit O.K. Corral and immerse yourself in the history of the famous gunfight.

3. Bird Cage Theatre

Bird Cage Theatre, located in Tombstone, Arizona, is a remarkable relic of the Old West. Built in 1881, this iconic establishment was a famous saloon, gambling den, and theater during its heyday. It gained a notorious reputation for its rowdy atmosphere and 24/7 operation, hosting a wide range of entertainment, from theater performances to boxing matches. Today, visitors can step back in time as they explore the well-preserved Bird Cage Theatre, marveling at the original decor, bullet holes in the walls, and the rich stories of its past, offering a fascinating glimpse into the Wild West's vibrant and sometimes lawless entertainment scene.

Location: 535 E Allen St, Tombstone, AZ 85638, USA

Closest City or Town: Douglas, AZ

How to Get There: To reach the Bird Cage Theatre, travel to Tombstone, Arizona, and locate the historic site in the town center. Choose your mode of transportation, whether driving or using public transit and follow signs leading to Tombstone.

GPS Coordinates: 31.7119° N, 110.0652° W

Best Time to Visit: Spring, Summer

Pass/Permit/fees: The ticket costs $14-$40.

Did you Know? You can explore its fascinating history.

WILLCOX

1. Chiricahua National Monument

Chiricahua National Monument, located in southeastern Arizona, is a stunning natural wonder that showcases the unique rock formations famous as the "Wonderland of Rocks." This national monument encompasses more than 11,000 acres of rugged terrain, with towering hoodoos, balanced rocks, and striking pinnacles sculpted by volcanic activity millions of years ago. Visitors can enjoy scenic hikes along the park's well-maintained trails, immersing themselves in the breathtaking beauty of this geological wonder. The monument also offers opportunities for camping, wildlife viewing, and stargazing, allowing nature enthusiasts to fully appreciate the diverse ecosystems and serene solitude of Chiricahua National Monument.

Location: 12856 East Rhyolite Creek Road, Willcox, AZ 85643, USA

Closest City or Town: Sierra, AZ

How to Get There: To get to Chiricahua National Monument, drive to the park using your vehicle or a rental car, following the designated roads and signs near Willcox, Arizona. Check the park's operating hours and visitor guidelines before your visit for a smooth experience.

GPS Coordinates: 32.0121° N, 109.3416° W

Best Time to Visit: Spring

Pass/Permit/fees: Entry is free.

Did you Know? It offers a wide range of activities.

BISBEE

1. Bisbee Mining & Historical Museum

The Bisbee Mining & Historical Museum is a captivating destination in the historic town of Bisbee, Arizona. This museum pays tribute to the town's rich mining heritage and comprehensively explores its history. Exhibits showcase the arduous work of miners, the development of mining technology, and the impact of mining on the community. Visitors can explore the underground mining world through guided tours and immersive displays. With its extensive collection of artifacts, photographs, and interactive exhibits, the Bisbee Mining & Historical Museum offers a fascinating journey into the past, illuminating the significance of mining in shaping Bisbee's identity.

Location: 5 Copper Queen Plaza, Bisbee, AZ 85603, USA

Closest City or Town: Sierra Vista, AZ

How to Get There: To reach the Bisbee Mining & Historical Museum, travel to Bisbee, Arizona, and locate the museum in the town's historic district. Choose your mode of transportation, whether driving or using public transit and follow signs leading to Bisbee.

GPS Coordinates: 31.4420° N, 109.9143° W

Best Time to Visit: Spring

Pass/Permit/fees: The ticket costs $10.

Did you Know? It is the best place to explore the rich mining history of Bisbee.

2. Copper Queen Mine

The Copper Queen Mine, located in Bisbee, Arizona, is a symbolic site that showcases the region's rich mining heritage. This historic mine played a crucial role in the growth and prosperity of the area. Today, visitors can embark on guided tours that take them deep into the mine's tunnels, providing a firsthand glimpse into the challenges and triumphs of underground mining. The tour guides, often former miners, share fascinating stories and insights, allowing visitors to appreciate the arduous work and the significant impact of the Copper Queen Mine on Bisbee's history and economy.

Location: Cochise County, Arizona, United States

Closest City or Town: Naco, Mexico

How to Get There: To get to the Copper Queen Mine in Bisbee, Arizona, travel to the town and locate the mine in the historic district. Choose your mode of transportation, whether driving or using public transit and follow signs leading to Bisbee.

GPS Coordinates: 31.4458° N, 109.9225° W

Best Time to Visit: Spring

Pass/Permit/fees: The ticket costs $14.

Did you Know? You can explore the area's rich mining history.

AJO

1. Organ Pipe Cactus National Monument

Organ Pipe Cactus National Monument is a breathtaking protected area in southern Arizona, USA. Spanning over 330,000 acres, it is renowned for its unique desert ecosystem and spectacular landscapes. The monument takes its name from the organ pipe cactus, a rare and majestic species that thrive in this region. The park offers various recreational activities, including hiking trails that wind through picturesque canyons, scenic drives showcasing stunning vistas, and camping opportunities to immerse oneself in the serene desert environment. Tourists can also explore the rich cultural heritage of the Tohono O'odham people, who have inhabited this land for centuries.

Location: 10 Organ Pipe Dr, Ajo, AZ 85321, USA

Closest City or Town: Buckeye, AZ

How to Get There: Organ Pipe Cactus National Monument is accessed via Arizona State Route 85, 150 miles southwest of Tucson and southeast of Yuma. Tucson International Airport (TUS) and Phoenix Sky Harbor International Airport (PHX) are the nearest major airports. Upon arrival, visitors can obtain permits and information at the monument's visitor centers.

GPS Coordinates: 32.0280° N, 112.8320° W

Best Time to Visit: December-January

Pass/Permit/fees: The ticket costs $25.

Did you Know? It is famous for its beauty and resilience of the desert landscape.

YUMA

1. Yuma Territorial Prison State Historic Park

Yuma Territorial Prison State Historical Park, located in Yuma, Arizona, is a captivating destination steeped in Wild West history. This former prison, operational from 1876 to 1909, housed many prisoners, including infamous outlaws. Today, the park offers a glimpse into the harsh conditions endured by inmates through well-preserved cell blocks, guard towers, and the dark "Dark Cell" solitary confinement area. Visitors can explore the museum, featuring artifacts and exhibits showcasing the prison's history. The park also hosts events, reenactments, and guided tours.

Location: 220 Prison Hill Rd, Yuma, AZ 85364, USA

Closest City or Town: Somerton, AZ

How to Get There: Yuma Territorial Prison State Historical Park is at 220 Prison Hill Road in Yuma, Arizona. It can be accessed by car via Interstate 10 and Exit 2 onto Giss Parkway. Visitors can pay the entrance fee at the visitor center and obtain information about the prison's history and exhibits.

GPS Coordinates: 32.7271° N, 114.6149° W

Best Time to Visit: November-March

Pass/Permit/fees: The ticket costs $10.

Did you Know? Visitors can immerse themselves in the intriguing tales of the Old West within the walls of Yuma Territorial Prison.

CAMP VERDE

1.   Montezuma Castle National Monument

Montezuma Castle National Monument, situated in central Arizona, is a beautiful testament to the ancient indigenous civilizations that once thrived in the region. This well-preserved cliff dwelling, built by the Sinagua people around 800 years ago, showcases the architectural ingenuity of its time. The five-story structure, nestled in a limestone cliff, features 20 rooms and serves as a dwelling for prehistoric farmers. Visitors can explore the monument through a self-guided trail that provides insights into the cultural significance and history of the site.

Location: Montezuma Castle Rd, Camp Verde, AZ, United States

Closest City or Town: Cottonwood, AZ

How to Get There: Montezuma Castle National Monument is located near Camp Verde, Arizona, and can be accessed by car via Interstate 17 and Exit 289. The nearest main airport is Phoenix Sky Harbor International Airport (PHX). Visitors can obtain information and permits at the visitor center upon arrival.

GPS Coordinates: 34.6116° N, 111.8350° W

Best Time to Visit: December-March

Pass/Permit/fees: The ticket costs $10. Kids under 15 are free.

Did you Know? It shows the rich Native American heritage and offers a fascinating glimpse into the past.

2.   Out of Africa Wildlife Park

Out of Africa Wildlife Park, located in Camp Verde, Arizona, is an extraordinary destination that offers an immersive wildlife experience. This unique park is home to a diverse range of exotic animals worldwide. Visitors can embark on thrilling safaris to witness up-close encounters with majestic lions, tigers, giraffes, and more. Educational and entertaining animal shows showcase the natural behaviors of the park's inhabitants. Additionally, interactive experiences allow guests to feed giraffes and even participate in a behind-the-scenes VIP tour. Out of Africa Wildlife Park provides a memorable and educational adventure for animal lovers of all ages.

Location: 3505 AZ-260, Camp Verde, AZ 86322, USA

Closest City or Town: Sedona, AZ

How to Get There: Out of Africa Wildlife Park is in Camp Verde, Arizona, at 3505 W State Route 260. It can be accessed by car via Interstate 17 and Exit 287 onto AZ-260.

GPS Coordinates: 34.6127° N, 111.9206° W

Best Time to Visit: March-October

Pass/Permit/fees: The ticket costs $28-$42. Kids under 3 are free.

Did you Know? You can enjoy a variety of experiences, including safaris, animal shows, and interactive encounters.

RIMROCK

1.   Montezuma Well National Monument

Montezuma Well National Monument near Rimrock, Arizona, is a captivating natural wonder that offers a glimpse into ancient Native American history. This natural limestone sinkhole contains a constant freshwater supply, forming a unique ecosystem. Visitors can explore the trails surrounding the well, marveling at the diverse flora and fauna that thrive in this oasis. The monument also features ancient cliff dwellings, evidence of past human habitation. Educational exhibits and ranger-led programs provide insights into the site's cultural significance. Montezuma Well National Monument is a serene and culturally rich destination, perfect for those seeking natural beauty and historical exploration.

Location: Forest Service Road 618, Rimrock, AZ 86335, USA

Closest City or Town: Sedona, AZ

How to Get There: Montezuma Well National Monument is near Rimrock, Arizona, off Montezuma Well Road. It can be reached by car via Interstate 17 and Exit 293 for McGuireville/Rimrock. A parking area is available for visitors, and access to the well and trails is accessible.

GPS Coordinates: 34.6489° N, 111.7552° W

Best Time to Visit: June- August

Pass/Permit/fees: The ticket costs $10. Kids under 15 are free.

Did you Know? It is famous for its beauty and history.

2.   V Bar V Heritage Site

V Bar V Heritage Site, situated near Sedona, Arizona, is a remarkable archaeological site that showcases ancient Native American rock art. This site, managed by the U.S. Forest Service, features one of the region's most extensive and best-preserved petroglyph panels. The intricate rock art, created by the Sinagua people over 1,000 years ago, depicts various symbols, animals, and human figures. Visitors can take a self-guided tour along a short trail to view and appreciate the remarkable petroglyphs. Interpretive panels provide insights into rock art's cultural significance and possible meanings, making V Bar V Heritage Site a fascinating and enriching destination for history and nature enthusiasts.

Location: 6750 Forest Service Rd 618, Rimrock, AZ 86335, USA

Closest City or Town: Cottonwood, AZ

How to Get There: V Bar V Heritage Site is near Sedona, Arizona, off Forest Road 618 (Beaver Creek Road). Visitors can reach the site by car via State Route 179. A parking area is available for visitors, and self-guided tours are offered along a designated trail.

GPS Coordinates: 34.6661° N, 111.7164° W

Best Time to Visit: Spring, Summer

Pass/Permit/fees: The ticket costs $5.

Did you Know? It is an ideal place for nature and heritage lovers.

Cottonwood

1. Historic Old Town Cottonwood

Historic Old Town Cottonwood, nestled in the heart of Arizona's Verde Valley, is a charming and vibrant destination steeped in rich history. This small town is renowned for its well-preserved historic district, unique shops, art galleries, and delightful restaurants. Visitors can admire the vintage buildings that exude old-world charm while strolling the streets. The town's thriving arts and culture scene and its picturesque location on the banks of the Verde River make it a perfect place to explore, indulge in local cuisine, discover local artists, and soak up the nostalgic ambiance of Historic Old Town Cottonwood.

Location: 281 N Main St, Cottonwood, AZ 86326, USA

Closest City or Town: Camp Verde, AZ

How to Get There: Historic Old Town Cottonwood is in central Arizona's Verde Valley, accessible via AZ-260 from Interstate

17. Visitors can explore the town's charming streets, lined with unique shops, art galleries, and restaurants. Ample parking is available, allowing for a delightful walk through the historic district.

GPS Coordinates: 34.7321° N, 112.0186° W

Best Time to Visit: Throughout the year.

Pass/Permit/fees: Entry is free

Did you Know? It is a treat to watch for history lovers.

2. Dead Horse Ranch State Park

Dead Horse Ranch State Park, nestled in the picturesque Verde Valley of Arizona, offers a serene escape into nature. This 423-acre park boasts a diverse landscape of cottonwood groves, lush green meadows, and the winding Verde River. Visitors can enjoy various outdoor activities, including hiking, biking, horseback riding, and fishing. The park also offers camping facilities, picnic areas, and a lagoon for birdwatching and water recreation. With its tranquil beauty and recreational opportunities, Dead Horse Ranch State Park is a haven for nature enthusiasts and a perfect destination for a day trip or camping getaway.

Location: 675 Dead Horse Ranch Rd, Cottonwood, AZ 86326, USA

Closest City or Town: Sedona, AZ

How to Get There: Dead Horse Ranch State Park is located in Cottonwood, Arizona, off AZ-260. It can be accessed by car via Interstate 17 and Exit 287.

GPS Coordinates: 34.7537° N, 112.0216° W

Best Time to Visit: Fall.

Pass/Permit/fees: The ticket costs $10.

Did you Know? It is famous for various outdoor activities, including hiking, biking, fishing, and camping.

3. Blazin' M Ranch

Blazing M Ranch, located in Cottonwood, Arizona, offers an authentic Western experience that immerses visitors in the spirit of the Old West. This Western-themed attraction invites guests to step back in time and enjoy various activities, including a hearty chuckwagon dinner, live entertainment featuring cowboy music and comedy, and an opportunity to explore the Ranch's Old West town. The Ranch also offers horse-drawn wagon rides, gold panning, and a shooting gallery, providing a fun-filled experience for the whole family. Blazin' M Ranch delivers a delightful blend of Western hospitality, entertainment, and Old West charm, making it a memorable destination for Western enthusiasts and those seeking a taste of cowboy culture.

Location: 1875 Mabery Ranch Rd, Cottonwood, AZ 86326, USA

Closest City or Town: Prescott Valley, AZ

How to Get There: Blazin' M Ranch is located in Cottonwood, Arizona, just off Highway 89A. Visitors can reach the Ranch by car via Interstate 17 and Exit 287. Ample parking is available.

GPS Coordinates: 34.7575° N, 112.0253° W

Best Time to Visit: Summer, Spring

Pass/Permit/fees: You can book tickets online.

Did you Know? It is a home of Western-themed activities and entertainment.

CLARKDALE

1.   Arizona Copper Art Museum

The Arizona Copper Art Museum is a captivating destination that celebrates copper's rich history and artistic beauty. The Clarkdale, Arizona museum showcases a stunning collection of copper artwork and artifacts. Visitors are immersed in copper craftsmanship, exploring intricate sculptures, jewelry, and exquisite decorative pieces. The museum also offers interactive exhibits that delve into the mining process and the significance of copper in Arizona's economy. Through its displays and educational programs, the Arizona Copper Art Museum highlights the cultural importance of copper while showcasing the incredible talent and skill of copper artists throughout history.

Location: 849 Main St, Clarkdale, AZ 86324, USA

Closest City or Town: Sedona, AZ

How to Get There: To visit the Arizona Copper Art Museum in Clarkdale, Arizona, plan your trip and check the museum's website for admission fees and operating hours. Arrive at the museum, purchase tickets if necessary, and explore the captivating exhibits showcasing the beauty and significance of copper art. Remember to visit the museum shop for unique copper souvenirs before leaving.

GPS Coordinates: 34.7711° N, 112.0568° W

Best Time to Visit: Throughout the year

Pass/Permit/fees: The ticket costs $5-$9.

Did you Know? It is a must-visit for anyone fascinated by the beauty and versatility of this unique metal.

JEROME

1. Jerome State Historic Park

Jerome State Historical Park, located in the historic town of Jerome, Arizona, offers visitors a glimpse into the town's intriguing past. Housed in the former Douglas Mansion, the park showcases exhibits depicting the town's rich mining history and the challenges its residents face. Visitors can explore the mansion's rooms, furnished with period pieces, photographs, and mining artifacts. The park also provides stunning panoramic views of the surrounding Verde Valley and an opportunity to learn about the geology and ecology of the region. With its fascinating exhibits and picturesque setting, Jerome State Historical Park is a must-visit for history enthusiasts and nature lovers.

Location: 100 Douglas Rd, Jerome, AZ 86331, USA

Closest City or Town: Cottonwood, AZ

How to Get There: To get to Jerome State Historical Park in Jerome, Arizona, plan your visit and find the best route to the town. Once in Jerome, follow the signage to locate the park within the former Douglas Mansion.

GPS Coordinates: 34.7536° N, 112.1112° W

Best Time to Visit: December-March

Pass/Permit/fees: You can book a ticket online.

Did you Know? You can enjoy the stunning views of the Verde Valley before continuing your journey.

VILLAGE OF OAK CREEK

1. Red Rock Scenic Byway (SR 179)

Red Rock Scenic Byway, also known as State Route 179, is a breathtaking drive through the mesmerizing landscapes of Sedona, Arizona. This 7.5-mile stretch of highway offers travelers panoramic vistas of majestic red rock formations, towering cliffs, and vibrant desert flora. The byway winds through iconic landmarks like Bell Rock, Cathedral Rock, and Courthouse Butte, providing numerous opportunities for photography, hiking, and immersing oneself in the region's natural beauty. With its awe-inspiring views and a blend of red rock wonders, the Red Rock Scenic Byway is a must-visit destination for nature enthusiasts and those seeking a scenic drive that captures the essence of Sedona.

Location: AZ-179 Arizona, USA

Closest City or Town: Sedona, AZ

How to Get There: To access the Red Rock Scenic Byway (SR 179) in Sedona, Arizona, plan your visit and find the best route to the city. Once in Sedona, follow the signs for SR 179, and drive along the scenic byway, enjoying the breathtaking views of red rock formations and natural beauty.

GPS Coordinates: 34.8377° N ,111.7924° W

Best Time to Visit: Summer, Spring

Pass/Permit/fees: Entry is free.

Did you Know? You can explore the attractions for an unforgettable experience.

SEDONA

1.   Palatki Ruins

The Palatki Ruins in Arizona offer a captivating journey into the ancient past. Nestled within the stunning red rock cliffs of Sedona, these cliff dwellings provide a glimpse into the lives of the Sinagua people who inhabited the area over 700 years ago. Visitors can explore the remarkably preserved ruins, which include pictographs, petroglyphs, and well-preserved structures. The site also features informative guided tours that delve into the Sinagua civilization's history, culture, and spirituality. With its rich archaeological significance and breathtaking natural surroundings, the Palatki Ruins are a must-visit destination for history enthusiasts and nature lovers alike.

Location: 10290 North Forest Service Road #795, Sedona, AZ 86336, USA

Closest City or Town: Cottonwood, AZ

How to Get There: To reach the Palatki Ruins in Arizona:

1.Plan your visit and find the best route to Sedona.

2.Once in Sedona, drive to the Coconino National Forest and follow Forest Road 525 (Boynton Pass Road) to the Palatki Heritage Site Visitor Center.

3.Check in at the center, join a guided tour, and explore it.

GPS Coordinates: 34 55' 4" N, 111 53' 59" W.

Best Time to Visit: Summer

Pass/Permit/fees: Different packages are available.

Did you Know? You can enjoy ancient cliff dwellings, pictographs, and petroglyphs for an immersive experience of the site's rich history.

2.   Amitabha Stupa & Peace Park

Amitabha Stupa & Peace Park, located in Sedona, Arizona, is a sacred sanctuary dedicated to peace, meditation, and spiritual rejuvenation. The stupa, a symbolic structure representing enlightenment, is a focal point of spiritual energy and tranquility. Surrounded by serene gardens and stunning red rock formations, the park offers visitors a peaceful atmosphere for reflection and contemplation. Whether you seek solace, inner peace, or a connection with the divine, the Amitabha Stupa & Peace Park invites you to immerse yourself in its tranquil ambiance, find comfort in its beauty, and experience a sense of harmony and serenity amidst the natural splendor of Sedona.

Location: 2650 Pueblo Dr, Sedona, AZ 86336, USA

Closest City or Town: Camp Verde, AZ

How to Get There: To reach the Amitabha Stupa & Peace Park in Sedona, Arizona, plan your visit and find the best route to the city. Once in Sedona, drive to the park located on Easy Street in West Sedona.

GPS Coordinates: 34.8756° N, 111.8083° W

Best Time to Visit: Summer

Pass/Permit/fees: Different packages are available.

Did you Know? You can have a peaceful atmosphere for a contemplative and rejuvenating experience.

3.   Doe Mountain Trail

The Doe Mountain Trail in Sedona, Arizona, offers an exhilarating outdoor adventure for hiking enthusiasts. This moderate to challenging trail takes you on a scenic journey up the iconic Doe Mountain, providing breathtaking panoramic views of the surrounding red rock landscape. As you ascend, you will navigate through rugged terrain, rocky outcrops, and vibrant vegetation, immersing yourself in the beauty of nature. Once you reach the summit, you will be rewarded with stunning vistas that stretch for miles, making it the perfect spot to capture memorable photographs or soak in the awe-inspiring scenery. The Doe Mountain Trail promises an unforgettable hiking experience in the heart of Sedona's natural wonders.

Location: Doe Mountain, Arizona 86336, USA

Closest City or Town: Flagstaff, AZ

How to Get There: To access the Doe Mountain Trail in Sedona, Arizona, plan your visit and find the best route to the city. Once in Sedona, locate Boynton Pass Road and follow the signs leading to the trailhead.

GPS Coordinates: 34.8822° N, 111.8921° W

Best Time to Visit: Summer

Pass/Permit/fees: Different packages are available.

Did you Know? It is the best place for a hike and enjoying the scenic views.

4.   Fay Canyon Trail

Fay Canyon Trail is a picturesque hiking trail in the Coconino National Forest near Sedona, Arizona. This trail offers a rewarding experience for nature lovers and outdoor adventurers. As you begin your journey, you will be greeted by towering red rock formations, lush vegetation, and breathtaking views of the surrounding canyon. The trail winds through a peaceful canyon shaded by tall trees, creating a serene atmosphere. Along the way, you may encounter a variety of wildlife and colorful wildflowers. The Fay Canyon Trail is a perfect choice for hikers seeking a moderate and family-friendly trek, providing an unforgettable encounter with Sedona's natural beauty.

Location: Fay Canyon Trail, Arizona 86336, USA

Closest City or Town: Prescott Valley, AZ

How to Get There: To get to Fay Canyon Trail in Sedona, Arizona, drive west on Highway 89A and turn north onto Dry Creek Road. After about 2 miles, turn right onto Boynton Pass Road and continue for 1.5 miles until you reach the trailhead on your right.

GPS Coordinates: 34.8884° N, 111.8578°

Best Time to Visit: Summer, Fall

Pass/Permit/fees: Different packages are available.

Did you Know? It is a scenic beauty of the red rock formations and tranquil canyon setting.

5. Cathedral Rock

Cathedral Rock is an iconic natural landmark in Sedona, Arizona, renowned for its majestic beauty and spiritual energy. This towering monolith captivates visitors with its awe-inspiring presence. The trail leading to Cathedral Rock offers a moderate challenge, rewarding hikers with breathtaking panoramic views of the Sedona landscape. The route takes you through stunning rock formations, narrow passages, and a final ascent that requires careful navigation. Once atop the summit, you are greeted with a breathtaking vista that encompasses the sprawling beauty of the area. Cathedral Rock is a must-visit destination for nature lovers and adventure seekers alike.

Location: Yavapai County, Arizona, U.S.

Closest City or Town: Prescott, AZ · Payson, AZ · Winslow, AZ

How to Get There: To get to Cathedral Rock in Sedona, Arizona, drive south on Highway 179 and turn left onto Back O' Beyond Road. After about 1.3 miles, you will reach the parking area for Cathedral Rock Trailhead.

GPS Coordinates: 34.8200° N, 111.7932° W

Best Time to Visit: Summer, Fall

Pass/Permit/fees: Different packages are available.

Did you Know? It offers captivating views of the surrounding red rock formations.

6. Snoopy Rock

Snoopy Rock is a distinctive rock formation located in Sedona, Arizona, known for its resemblance to the iconic cartoon character Snoopy lying on top of his doghouse. This natural wonder has become a beloved regional symbol and a popular visitor attraction. The rock formation stands tall amidst the picturesque red rocks, offering a whimsical and playful sight. Hikers and nature enthusiasts can enjoy the view of Snoopy Rock from various vantage points and nearby trails. It is a delightful spot to capture photos, appreciates Sedona's unique formations, and indulge in the imagination that the rock's resemblance evokes.

Location: Sedona, AZ 86336, USA

Closest City or Town: Payson, AZ · Winslow, AZ

How to Get There: To get to Snoopy Rock in Sedona, Arizona, drive north on Highway 89A and turn right onto Dry Creek Road. After approximately 1 mile, you will spot the distinctive Snoopy Rock formation on your left.

GPS Coordinates: 34.8603° N, 111.7516° W

Best Time to Visit: October-November

Pass/Permit/fees: Different packages are available.

Did you Know? It is an iconic landmark amidst Sedona's beautiful red rock scenery.

7. Crescent Moon Picnic Site

Crescent Moon Picnic Site, located in Sedona, Arizona, is a scenic and serene spot nestled along the banks of Oak Creek. This picturesque site offers a delightful setting for picnicking, relaxation, and outdoor recreation. Surrounded by towering red rock cliffs and shaded by lush vegetation, visitors can unwind in the tranquility of nature. The picnic area features shaded tables, BBQ grills, and restroom facilities, providing all the amenities needed for a comfortable outing. Moreover, it serves as a gateway to iconic hiking trails such as Cathedral Rock, making it a perfect starting point for exploring the mesmerizing beauty of Sedona's natural wonders.

Location: 333 Red Rock Crossing Rd, Sedona, AZ 86336, United States

Closest City or Town: Winslow, AZ

How to Get There: To get to Crescent Moon Picnic Site in Sedona, Arizona, drive south on Highway 179 until you see the sign for the picnic site on your right. Turn right and follow the road to the parking area.

GPS Coordinates: 34.8266° N, 111.8071° W

Best Time to Visit: Fall, Spring

Pass/Permit/fees: The ticket costs $ 11.

Did you Know? It is stunning red rock scenery.

8. Bell Rock

Bell Rock is a majestic and iconic rock formation in Sedona, Arizona. It stands prominently, resembling a massive bell rising from the desert landscape. This stunning landmark attracts visitors worldwide, offering breathtaking views and awe. The trail leading to Bell Rock provides a memorable hiking experience, allowing adventurers to explore its unique features up close. Whether admiring it from a distance or venturing on the trail, Bell Rock captivates with its towering presence and vibrant red hues, leaving a lasting impression on all who witness its grandeur.

Location: Yavapai, Arizona, U.S.

Closest City or Town: Winslow, AZ

How to Get There: To get to Bell Rock in Sedona, Arizona, drive south on Highway 179 and turn right onto Bell Rock Boulevard. After approximately 0.5 miles, you will reach the parking area for Bell Rock Trailhead.

GPS Coordinates: 34.8003° N, 111.7646° W

Best Time to Visit: Fall, Spring

Pass/Permit/fees: Different packages are available.

Did you Know? You can enjoy the stunning views of Bell Rock and the surrounding red rock formations.

9. Soldier Pass (Brin's Mesa)

Soldier Pass, also known as Brin's Mesa, is a beautiful hiking trail in the heart of Sedona, Arizona. This scenic trek offers a mesmerizing journey through rugged terrain, ancient rock formations, and breathtaking vistas. As hikers traverse the trail, they are treated to sweeping panoramas of the red rock landscape punctuated by the iconic buildings of the Sedona region. Soldier Pass is renowned for its enchanting natural beauty, including the famous Devil's Kitchen sinkhole and the picturesque Seven Sacred Pools. With its rich history, geological wonders, and awe-inspiring views, Soldier Pass beckons adventurers seeking an unforgettable experience in Sedona's majestic wilderness.

Location: Soldier Pass Trail & Brins Mesa Trail, Arizona 86336, USA.

Closest City or Town: Cottonwood, AZ.

How to Get There: Soldier Pass Trail & Brins Mesa Trail Arizona 86336, USA

To reach Soldier Pass (Brin's Mesa) in Sedona, Arizona, drive west on Highway 89A, take Soldiers Pass Road, and park at the trailhead.

GPS Coordinates: 34.879167° N, 111.786667° W

Best Time to Visit: Spring

Pass/Permit/fees: The ticket costs $5-$15.

Did you Know? You can enjoy breathtaking views here.

10. Devil's Bridge Trail

The Devil's Bridge Trail is a captivating hiking adventure in Sedona, Arizona. This trail offers a thrilling journey through stunning red rock landscapes. As hikers navigate the path, they encounter breathtaking vistas and fascinating geological formations. The trail's highlight is Devil's Bridge, a natural sandstone arch standing tall amidst the scenic beauty. Brave souls can walk across the bridge for a unique and awe-inspiring experience. With its natural wonders, exhilarating hike, and the chance to stand on the majestic Devil's Bridge, this trail leaves visitors with unforgettable memories of Sedona's enchanting wilderness.

Location: Devil's Bridge Trail, Arizona 86336, USA

Closest City or Town: Camp Verde, AZ.

How to Get There: To get to Devil's Bridge Trail in Sedona, Arizona, drive west on Highway 89A, turn onto Dry Creek Road, and continue until you reach Forest Road 152. Take Forest Road 152 for approximately 1.5 miles to the designated parking area.

GPS Coordinates: 34.9000° N, 111.8267° W

Best Time to Visit: Spring, Fall

Pass/Permit/fees: The ticket costs $5-$15.

Did you Know? It is famous for its beauty.

11. Oak Creek Canyon

Oak Creek Canyon, located in northern Arizona, is a natural wonder that enchants visitors with its breathtaking beauty. Carved over millennia by the flowing waters of Oak Creek, this canyon offers a mesmerizing landscape of towering red rock cliffs, lush green forests, and crystal-clear streams. Traveling along the scenic State Route 89A, visitors are treated to panoramic vistas, cascading waterfalls, hiking, camping, and picnicking opportunities. Oak Creek Canyon is a haven for nature lovers, providing a serene escape from the bustling world as they immerse themselves in the tranquility and splendor of this remarkable canyon.

Location: Sedona, AZ 86336, United States

Closest City or Town: Flagstaff, AZ.

How to Get There: To reach Oak Creek Canyon in Arizona, drive south on Interstate 17 from Flagstaff. Take Exit 337 onto Highway 89A, and continue for about 25 miles until you enter the scenic Oak Creek Canyon.

GPS Coordinates: 34.9125° N, 111.7268° W

Best Time to Visit: Fall

Pass/Permit/fees: The ticket costs $8.

Did you Know? You can explore attractions like Slide Rock State Park.

12. Airport Mesa

Airport Mesa, located in Sedona, Arizona, is a captivating destination renowned for its panoramic views and spiritual allure. This stunning mesa offers a unique vantage point to admire the surrounding red rock formations and the picturesque Sedona landscape. The highlight of Airport Mesa is the Airport Vortex, believed by many to possess energy centers that promote healing and spiritual connection. Visitors can hike to the top of the mesa, where a designated viewpoint provides breathtaking vistas of Sedona's iconic landmarks. Whether seeking tranquility, inspiration, or simply the beauty of nature, a visit to Airport Mesa is a must for any Sedona adventure.

Location: 483 Airport Rd, Sedona, AZ 86336, USA

Closest City or Town: Chino Valley, AZ.

How to Get There: To get to Airport Mesa in Sedona, Arizona, drive west on Highway 89A, turn onto Airport Road, and continue until you reach the parking area.

GPS Coordinates: 34.8558° N, 111.7801° W

Best Time to Visit: Throughout the year

Pass/Permit/fees: Entry is free.

Did you Know? Airport Mesa is a must for any Sedona adventure.

13. Slide Rock State Park

Slide Rock State Park, nestled in Oak Creek Canyon near Sedona, Arizona, is a natural playground that beckons visitors with its unique attractions. The park is famous for its smooth, natural water slides formed by the creek cascading over slick sandstone surfaces. Adventurers of all ages can slide down these exhilarating chutes, plunging into refreshing pools below. The park also offers opportunities for swimming, picnicking, hiking along scenic trails, and simply basking in the stunning beauty of the canyon. With its thrilling water slides and picturesque surroundings, Slide Rock State Park promises a memorable and fun-filled day in Arizona's natural splendor.

Location: Arizona 86336, USA

Closest City or Town: Payson, AZ.

How to Get There: To reach Slide Rock State Park in Oak Creek Canyon near Sedona, Arizona, drive north on Highway 89A for approximately 7 miles.

GPS Coordinates: 34.9436° N, 111.7529° W

Best Time to Visit: Summer, Fall

Pass/Permit/fees: The ticket costs $5- $10.

Did you Know? You can enjoy the natural waterslides, pools, and surrounding amenities.

14. Chapel of the Holy Cross

The Chapel of the Holy Cross, located in Sedona, Arizona, is a breathtaking architectural marvel that blends seamlessly with its natural surroundings. This iconic spiritual sanctuary offers panoramic views of the majestic red rock formations and the vast expanse of the valley below. Designed by renowned architect Marguerite Brunswig Staude, the chapel's design exemplifies a harmonious fusion of modernist principles and the awe-inspiring beauty of the natural landscape. Visitors are drawn to the serenity and spiritual energy that permeates the chapel, making it a revered destination for contemplation, reflection, and connecting with the divine amidst the captivating splendor of Sedona.

Location: 780 Chapel Rd, Sedona, AZ 86336, USA

Closest City or Town: Cottonwood, AZ.

How to Get There: To reach the Chapel of the Holy Cross in Sedona, Arizona, drive south on Highway 179 for approximately 3.5 miles. Look for the entrance on the right-hand side and follow Chapel Road to the designated parking areas.

GPS Coordinates: 34.8320° N, 111.7668° W

Best Time to Visit: Winter

Pass/Permit/fees: Entry is free.

Did you Know? You can enjoy the breathtaking views.

15. Red Rock State Park

Red Rock State Park, nestled in the heart of Sedona, Arizona, is a natural haven that showcases the stunning beauty of the red rock formations. This park offers diverse trails that wind through lush greenery along the banks of Oak Creek and amidst towering red rock cliffs. Visitors can immerse themselves in the tranquility of nature, observe local wildlife, and marvel at the geological wonders. The park also serves as an educational hub, providing insights into the region's unique ecosystem and cultural history. Red Rock State Park is a must-visit destination for nature enthusiasts seeking solace in the captivating landscapes of Sedona.

Location: 4050 Red Rock Loop Rd, Sedona, AZ 86336, USA

Closest City or Town: Payson, AZ.

How to Get There: To reach the Chapel of the Holy Cross in Sedona, Arizona, drive south on Highway 179 for approximately 3.5 miles. Look for the entrance on the right-hand side and follow Chapel Road to the designated parking areas.

GPS Coordinates: 34.8129° N, 111.8306° W

Best Time to Visit: Summer

Pass/Permit/fees: The ticket costs $10.

Did you Know? You can explore the diverse landscapes and enjoy the scenic views.

16. Sedona Airport Overlook

Sedona Airport Overlook is a mesmerizing destination in Sedona, Arizona's enchanting red rock country. This scenic viewpoint offers breathtaking panoramic views of the natural wonders. The overlook gives visitors a unique vantage point to marvel at the stunning red sandstone formations, including the iconic Cathedral Rock and Bell Rock and the verdant valleys below. It is a popular spot for photographers, nature enthusiasts, and hikers who seek to capture the awe-inspiring beauty of Sedona's landscape. The tranquility of the location, coupled with the vibrant colors and dramatic cliffs, creates an unforgettable experience for anyone who ventures to Sedona Airport Overlook.

Location: 538 Airport Rd, Sedona, AZ 86336, USA

Closest City or Town: Chino Valley, AZ.

How to Get There: Sedona Airport Overlook, in Arizona's red rock country, offers stunning panoramic views of Cathedral Rock and Bell Rock. Follow AZ-89A to the roundabout, take the second exit onto Airport Road, and continue uphill to the parking lot.

GPS Coordinates: 34.8129° N, 111.8306° W

Best Time to Visit: Throughout the year

Pass/Permit/fees: Entry is free.

Did you Know? You can enjoy the captivating Sedona Airport Overlook.

17. Broken Arrow Trail

Broken Arrow Trail is a beautiful hiking trail in Sedona, Arizona, renowned for its breathtaking beauty and exhilarating adventure. This moderate-level trail offers a mesmerizing journey through stunning red rock formations, towering cliffs, and enchanting desert landscapes. The track is famous for its iconic landmarks like Chicken Point and Submarine Rock, which provide awe-inspiring views of the surrounding scenery. Adventurers can also witness the thrill of navigating rugged terrain and encountering natural obstacles, making it a favorite among off-road enthusiasts. With its natural splendor and thrilling exploration blend, Broken Arrow

Trail promises an unforgettable outdoor experience in Sedona's mesmerizing red rock country.

Location: Broken Arrow Trail, Arizona 86336, USA

Closest City or Town: Cottonwood, AZ.

How to Get There: To reach the Broken Arrow Trail in Sedona, Arizona, drive south on AZ-179 from the "Y" roundabout for about 3.3 miles. Turn left onto Morgan Road and continue for approximately 1.3 miles until you see the signage for the Broken Arrow Trailhead on your right.

GPS Coordinates: 34.8455° N, 111.7569° W

Best Time to Visit: March-May

Pass/Permit/fees: The ticket costs $25-$50.

Did you Know? It is famous for hiking.

18.   West Fork Oak Creek Trail

West Fork Oak Creek Trail is a beautiful hiking trail in the heart of Sedona, Arizona. Renowned for its scenic beauty, this trail meanders alongside the crystal-clear waters of Oak Creek, offering a serene and picturesque experience. Hikers are immersed in a lush canyon adorned with vibrant foliage, towering cliffs, and fascinating rock formations. As you traverse the trail, you will cross the creek multiple times, adding an element of adventure to the journey. With its tranquil ambiance and breathtaking surroundings, West Fork Oak Creek Trail is a must-visit destination for nature lovers seeking a peaceful escape in Sedona's stunning wilderness.

Location: W Fork Trail, Sedona, AZ 86336, USA

Closest City or Town: Payson, AZ.

How to Get There: To reach the West Fork Oak Creek Trail in Sedona, Arizona, follow AZ-89A northbound for approximately 9.5 miles until you see the entrance on the right-hand side. Look for the sign indicating the trailhead and parking area.

GPS Coordinates: 34.9906° N, 111.7431° W

Best Time to Visit: April-October

Pass/Permit/fees: The ticket costs $11.

Did you Know? It offers breathtaking views of the surrounding canyon.

19.   Boynton Canyon Trail

Boynton Canyon Trail is a scenic hiking trail in the heart of Sedona, Arizona. This trail offers a breathtaking adventure for outdoor enthusiasts. The trail winds through a majestic red rock canyon, surrounded by towering cliffs and lush vegetation. Along the way, hikers are treated to stunning panoramic views of the surrounding landscape, including iconic rock formations like the Kachina Woman and the Boynton Canyon Vortex. The trail also leads to the ruins of ancient Native American dwellings, adding a touch of history and intrigue to the experience. With its natural beauty and cultural significance, Boynton Canyon Trail is a must-visit destination for nature lovers seeking serenity and exploration.

Location: Boynton Cyn Trl Arizona 86336, USA

Closest City or Town: Payson, AZ.

How to Get There: To reach Boynton Canyon Trail, head to Sedona, Arizona, and drive to the intersection of Highway 89A and Dry Creek Road. Take a right onto Boynton Pass Road and drive for about 1.5 miles until you reach the well-marked trailhead parking area.

GPS Coordinates: 34.9074° N, 111.8485° W

Best Time to Visit: Summer

Pass/Permit/fees: You can book a ticket online.

Did you Know? It is a perfect place to hike and enjoy the beauty of the Boynton Canyon.

PRESCOTT

1.   Sharlot Hall Museum

The Sharlot Hall Museum is a captivating historical museum in Prescott, Arizona. Named after Sharlot M. Hall, a prominent Arizona pioneer, writer, and historian, the museum showcases the region's rich cultural heritage. Spanning over four acres, it consists of multiple historic buildings, including the Governor's Mansion, Fort Misery, and the Ranch House. Visitors can explore exhibits featuring Native American artifacts, pioneer history, and territorial-era displays. The museum also hosts various events, festivals, and educational programs throughout the year, offering visitors a deeper understanding of Arizona's past. With its immersive exhibits and engaging programming, the Sharlot Hall Museum is a must-visit destination for history enthusiasts and curious minds alike.

Location: 415 W Gurley St, Prescott, AZ 86301, USA

Closest City or Town: Sedona, AZ.

How to Get There: To reach the Sharlot Hall Museum in Prescott, Arizona, head to the intersection of Gurley Street and Montezuma Street in downtown Prescott. Look for the museum at 415 W. Gurley Street, and find nearby parking in public lots or on the street.

GPS Coordinates: 34.5417° N, 112.4732° W

Best Time to Visit: Throughout the year.

Pass/Permit/fees: The ticket costs $10- $12.

Did you Know? You can explore the fascinating history of the museum's historic buildings.

2.   Lynx Lake Recreation Area

The Lynx Lake Recreation Area is a picturesque haven in Prescott National Forest, Arizona. Spanning over 300 acres, it offers many outdoor activities and stunning natural surroundings. The area's centerpiece is the serene Lynx Lake, where visitors can enjoy boating, fishing, and kayaking. The surrounding trails provide ample hiking, mountain biking, and bird-watching opportunities, with breathtaking views of the lake and surrounding forest. Additionally, the recreation area features picnic areas, campgrounds, and a visitor center, ensuring a memorable and enjoyable experience for nature lovers and outdoor enthusiasts of all ages.

Location: Lynx Lake Store Rd, Prescott, AZ 86303, United States

Closest City or Town: Camp Verde, AZ.

How to Get There: To get to the Lynx Lake Recreation Area in Prescott, Arizona, drive east on Gurley Street until you reach the intersection with Mount Vernon Avenue. Take a right onto Mount Vernon Avenue and continue for about 2 miles until you see the entrance to the recreation area on your right.

GPS Coordinates: 34.5218° N, 112.3842° W

Best Time to Visit: March-February.

Pass/Permit/fees: The ticket costs $5.

Did you Know? You can enjoy the various activities and amenities offered at Lynx Lake.

3. Watson Lake

Watson Lake is a stunning reservoir in Prescott, Arizona's Granite Dells region. With its unique rock formations and crystal-clear waters, Watson Lake offers a picturesque escape for outdoor enthusiasts. Visitors can enjoy various activities, such as boating, kayaking, fishing, and hiking along the lake's scenic trails. The iconic granite boulders dot the landscape and provide a dramatic backdrop for photography and exploration. Additionally, the park features picnic areas, a campground, and opportunities for wildlife viewing.

Location: Granite Dells, Prescott, Arizona,

Closest City or Town: Chino Valley, AZ.

How to Get There: To get to Watson Lake in Prescott, Arizona, drive north on State Route 89 until you reach the roundabout at Willow Creek Road. Take the first exit onto Willow Creek Road and continue for about 4 miles. Look for signs for Watson Lake Park, turn right onto Watson Lake Park Road, and follow it to the park entrance.

GPS Coordinates: 34.5875° N, 112.4180° W

Best Time to Visit: Summer.

Pass/Permit/fees: The ticket costs $3.

Did you Know? It is a captivating destination showcasing Arizona's natural beauty.

FLAGSTAFF

1. Flagstaff Visitor Center

The Flagstaff Visitor Center serves as a welcoming gateway to the enchanting city of Flagstaff, Arizona. Nestled amidst the breathtaking beauty of the Coconino National Forest and the San Francisco Peaks, the center provides a wealth of information and resources for tourists and travelers. With a team of knowledgeable and friendly staff, visitors can obtain guidance on attractions, outdoor activities, and local events. The center offers maps, brochures, and insider tips to help visitors maximize their stay. Whether seeking adventure in the nearby Grand Canyon or exploring Flagstaff's vibrant downtown, the Flagstaff Visitor Center is an invaluable resource for an unforgettable experience in this picturesque mountain town.

Location: 1 E Rte 66, Flagstaff, AZ 86001, USA

Closest City or Town: Winslow, AZ.

How to Get There: The Flagstaff Visitor Center is at 1 E. Route 66, Flagstaff, AZ 86001. You can easily reach it by car via Interstate 40 or State Route 89. If you prefer public transportation, the Mountain Line bus system offers routes to the downtown area where the Visitor Center is situated.

GPS Coordinates: 35.1974° N, 111.6492° W

Best Time to Visit: September- October.

Pass/Permit/fees: You can book a ticket online.

Did you Know? It is famous for its beauty.

2. Museum of Northern Arizona

The Museum of Northern Arizona in Flagstaff is a captivating institution that celebrates the Colorado Plateau region's rich cultural and natural heritage. With its striking architecture nestled amidst the Ponderosa pine forest, the museum houses an extensive collection of Native American art and artifacts. It exhibits that showcase the diverse indigenous cultures of the area. Visitors can explore exhibits on geology, biology, anthropology, and fine art, providing a comprehensive understanding of the region's past and present. The museum also hosts educational programs, festivals, and lectures that foster a deeper appreciation for the unique landscapes and cultures of Northern Arizona.

Location: 3101 N Fort Valley Rd, Flagstaff, AZ 86001, USA

Closest City or Town: Prescott Valley, AZ.

How to Get There: The Museum of Northern Arizona is at 3101 N. Fort Valley Road, Flagstaff, AZ 86001. It can be reached by car via US-180 N/Fort Valley Road or public transportation with the Mountain Line bus system. Taxis and ride-sharing services are also available for convenient transportation to the museum.

GPS Coordinates: 35.2345° N, 111.6656° W

Best Time to Visit: June-September.

Pass/Permit/fees: The ticket costs $15.

Did you Know? It is a home of American art?

3.   Riordan Mansion State Historic Park

Riordan Mansion State Historical Park, nestled in Flagstaff, Arizona, offers a captivating glimpse into the rich history of the Riordan family and the region's architectural heritage. This beautifully preserved Arts and Crafts-style mansion was built in 1904 and showcases exquisite craftsmanship and design. Visitors can take guided tours through the mansion's elegant rooms, filled with original furnishings and decor. The park also features informative exhibits, hiking trails, and picnic areas, allowing visitors to immerse themselves in the natural beauty that surrounds the mansion. Riordan Mansion State Historical Park is a testament to Flagstaff's past and a must-visit destination for history enthusiasts.

Location: 409 W Riordan Rd, Flagstaff, AZ 86001, USA

Closest City or Town: Prescott, AZ.

How to Get There: Riordan Mansion State Historic Park is at 409 W Riordan Road, Flagstaff, AZ 86001. You can reach the park by car, heading west on W Route 66 and turning left onto N Humphreys Street, then right onto W Riordan Road. The park is also accessible by public transportation through the Mountain Line bus system, and taxi or ride-sharing services are also available.

GPS Coordinates: 35.1874° N, 111.6595° W

Best Time to Visit: Summer.

Pass/Permit/fees: The ticket costs $2.

Did you Know?   It is famous for its history.

4.   Flagstaff Extreme

Flagstaff Extreme is an exhilarating outdoor adventure park nestled in the stunning forests of Flagstaff, Arizona. This high-flying attraction offers a thrilling experience for adventure enthusiasts of all ages. With an array of challenging obstacle courses and zipline circuits, visitors can test their skills, push their limits, and embrace their sense of adventure. Each track offers a unique and adrenaline-pumping challenge, from navigating swinging logs to traversing rope bridges suspended among the treetops. Flagstaff Extreme provides a safe and exciting environment, allowing participants to enjoy the natural beauty of the forest while embarking on an unforgettable aerial adventure.

Location: Fort Tuthill County Park, 2446 Ft Tuthill Lp, Flagstaff, AZ 86005, USA

Closest City or Town: Chino Valley, AZ.

How to Get There: Flagstaff Extreme is at 1800 S. Woody Mountain Road, Flagstaff, AZ 86001. You can reach it by car, heading south on Milton Road, turning left onto Butler Avenue, and continuing onto Woody Mountain Road. Unfortunately, public transportation does not directly serve Flagstaff Extreme, but taxi or ride-sharing services are available for convenient transportation to the park.

GPS Coordinates: 35.1429° N, 111.6923° W

Best Time to Visit: September- October

Pass/Permit/fees: The ticket costs $60.

Did you Know?   It is famous for adventure.

5.   Lava River Cave

Lava River Cave, located near Flagstaff, Arizona, is a mesmerizing underground wonder that draws adventurers seeking an extraordinary experience. This lava tube cave, formed thousands of years ago by volcanic activity, offers a unique glimpse into the region's geological history. Exploring the cave entails a narrow, dark journey through its vast chambers adorned with fascinating rock formations and eerie silence. Visitors are encouraged to bring sturdy footwear, flashlights, and a sense of adventure to traverse the lava-covered floor. The Lava River Cave provides an awe-inspiring and otherworldly experience for those willing to venture into its mysterious depths.

Location: 171B Forest Rd, Flagstaff, AZ 86001, USA

Closest City or Town: Payson, AZ.

How to Get There: Lava River Cave near Flagstaff, Arizona, is accessed by driving west on US-180/N Fort Valley Road and turning right onto Forest Road 245/Lava River Cave Road. Public transportation does not directly serve the cave, so having your vehicle or using a taxi or ride-sharing service is recommended.

GPS Coordinates: 35.3424° N, 111.8363° W

Best Time to Visit: Summer

Pass/Permit/fees: Entry is free.

Did you Know? Visitors can explore its beautiful underground passages?

6. Coconino National Forest

Coconino National Forest, located in northern Arizona, is a breathtaking and diverse natural wonderland that spans over 1.8 million acres. With its awe-inspiring landscapes, including towering ponderosa pine forests, deep canyons, and dramatic red rock formations, the forest offers endless opportunities for outdoor enthusiasts. Hiking trails, camping sites, and scenic drives abound, immersing visitors in the region's natural beauty. Notable attractions within the forest include the iconic Oak Creek Canyon, picturesque Sedona, and the historic Route 66. Coconino National Forest is a haven for adventure, tranquility, and exploration, beckoning visitors to discover its extraordinary wonders.

Location: Lake Mary Rd, Flagstaff, AZ 86001, USA

Closest City or Town: Sedona, AZ.

How to Get There: Coconino National Forest in northern Arizona is accessible by car via major highways such as Interstate 17, Interstate 40, and State Route 89. Public transportation options to specific areas within the forest may be limited, so renting a car or using a taxi or ride-sharing service is recommended.

GPS Coordinates: 34.9132° N, 111.5591° W

Best Time to Visit: October

Pass/Permit/fees: The ticket costs $ 20.

Did you Know? You can enjoy the vast and diverse landscape of Coconino National Forest?

7. Walnut Canyon National Monument

Walnut Canyon National Monument, located near Flagstaff, Arizona, is a remarkable testament to ancient civilizations and natural beauty. The monument is renowned for its stunning cliff dwellings, where the Sinagua people lived over 700 years ago. Visitors can embark on a scenic hike along the rim or descend into the canyon to explore the well-preserved dwellings. The sheer limestone walls and panoramic vistas create a captivating backdrop, offering glimpses into the lives and ingenuity of the past inhabitants. Walnut Canyon National Monument is a window to the past, inviting visitors to connect with history and marvel at the extraordinary landscape.

Location: Arizona, USA

Closest City or Town: Chino Valley, AZ.

How to Get There: Walnut Canyon National Monument is 10 miles southeast of Flagstaff, Arizona. To get there, take I-40 eastbound from downtown Flagstaff and use Exit 204 towards the monument. Public transportation does not directly serve the memorial, so having your vehicle or using a taxi or ride-sharing service is recommended for transport.

GPS Coordinates: 35.1690° N, 111.5043° W

Best Time to Visit: March

Pass/Permit/fees: The ticket costs $15.

Did you Know? It is an ideal place to learn about ancient civilization?

8. Sunset Crater Volcano National Monument

Sunset Crater Volcano National Monument near Flagstaff, Arizona, is a beautiful testament to the area's volcanic past. The monument showcases the remains of an ancient volcanic eruption that occurred nearly a millennium ago, leaving behind a stunning landscape of lava flows, cinder cones, and colorful volcanic ash. Visitors can explore the trails that wind through the unique terrain, offering panoramic views and insights into the region's geologic history. The monument's centerpiece, Sunset Crater, with its vivid hues and dramatic contours, reminds us of the dynamic forces that shaped the landscape.

Location: 6082 Sunset Crater Road, Flagstaff, AZ 86004, USA

Closest City or Town: Sedona, AZ.

How to Get There: Sunset Crater Volcano National Monument is 12 miles north of Flagstaff, Arizona. To get there, take US-89 northbound from downtown Flagstaff and follow the signs to the monument's entrance. Public transportation does not directly serve the memorial, so having your vehicle or using a taxi or ride-sharing service is recommended for transport.

GPS Coordinates: 35.3711° N, 111.5108° W

Best Time to Visit: Spring, Summer, Fall

Pass/Permit/fees: The ticket costs $15.

Did you Know? It offers a mesmerizing experience for nature enthusiasts and history buffs?

9. Wupatki National Monument

Wupatki National Monument, situated in northern Arizona, showcases the remarkable ruins of ancient Puebloan settlements. The monument encompasses over 35,000 acres of desert landscape, featuring impressive multistory masonry structures and evidence of human habitation dating back over 900 years. Visitors can explore the interconnected communities, marvel at the intricate architecture, and learn about the vibrant history and culture of the people who once thrived here. Additionally, the monument offers scenic viewpoints, hiking trails, and opportunities for birdwatching.

Location: Flagstaff, AZ 86004, USA

Closest City or Town: Payson, AZ.

How to Get There: Wupatki National Monument is approximately 40 miles northeast of Flagstaff, Arizona. To get there, take US-89 northbound and turn right onto Wupatki Loop Road. Public transportation does not directly serve the monument, so having your vehicle or using a taxi or ride-sharing service is recommended for transport.

GPS Coordinates: 35.5600° N, 111.3935° W

Best Time to Visit: Throughout the year.

Pass/Permit/fees: The ticket costs $25.

Did you Know? You can enjoy the unique natural and cultural heritage of Wupatki National Monument?

10. Lowell Observatory

Lowell Observatory, nestled in Flagstaff, Arizona, is a renowned astronomical research facility and a hub of scientific exploration. Founded in 1894, it boasts a rich history of groundbreaking discoveries, including identifying Pluto. Visitors can embark on guided tours that showcase historic telescopes, astronomical artifacts, and engaging exhibits. Stargazing programs allow one to observe celestial wonders through telescopes and learn from knowledgeable astronomers. The observatory's dedication to education and public outreach makes it an ideal destination for astronomy enthusiasts of all ages.

Location: 1400 W Mars Hill Rd, Flagstaff, AZ 86001, USA

Closest City or Town: Payson, AZ.

How to Get There: Lowell Observatory is located in Flagstaff, Arizona, west of downtown. From downtown Flagstaff, you can head west on W Route 66 and continue onto W Santa Fe Avenue to reach the observatory. Public transportation options, such as local buses or taxi/ride-sharing services, may be available to access Lowell Observatory.

GPS Coordinates: 35.2029° N, 111.6646° W

Best Time to Visit: Throughout the year.

Pass/Permit/fees: The ticket costs $29.

Did you Know? It offers a chance to delve into the wonders of the universe and the pioneering spirit of scientific inquiry.

WILLIAMS

1. Williams Depot

Williams Depot, located in Williams, Arizona, is a historic train station, the gateway to the Grand Canyon. Built-in 1908, the depot exudes a charming old-world ambiance and offers a nostalgic journey back in time. It is the departure point for the Grand Canyon Railway, a scenic train ride that takes passengers on a breathtaking journey to the South Rim of the Grand Canyon. The depot features a gift shop, restaurant, and friendly staff ready to assist visitors in planning their Grand Canyon adventure. Williams Depot is not just a transportation hub but also a destination that adds a touch of nostalgia and excitement to any Grand Canyon exploration.

Location: 233 N Grand Canyon Blvd, Williams, AZ 86046, USA

Closest City or Town: Flagstaff, AZ.

How to Get There: Williams Depot is located in Williams, Arizona, conveniently accessible from Interstate 40 (I-40). If driving, take Exit 163 and follow the signs to Williams. Alternatively, take the scenic Grand Canyon Railway from the depot to Williams. Public transportation options may be available, so it is worth checking local bus services for routes passing or near the depot.

GPS Coordinates: 35.2514° N, 112.1907° W

Best Time to Visit: Spring -Fall.

Pass/Permit/fees: Different packages are available.

Did you Know? It is a perfect place for hangouts?

2. Grand Canyon Deer Farm

The Grand Canyon Deer Farm is a unique and enchanting attraction near the majestic Grand Canyon in Williams, Arizona. Spanning over ten acres of picturesque land, visitors can get up close and personal with various beautiful deer species. As you stroll through the farm, you will be greeted by gentle deer roaming freely, creating an immersive and unforgettable experience. The farm provides a safe environment for both the animals and the visitors, with knowledgeable staff offering insights into the behavior and characteristics of these magnificent creatures.

Location: 6769 Deer Farm Rd, Williams, AZ 86046, USA

Closest City or Town: Sedona, AZ.

How to Get There: To reach the Grand Canyon Deer Farm, travel to Williams, Arizona, and follow GPS directions to 6769 E Deer Farm Road. Enjoy an immersive experience with graceful deer species, following the farm's staff guidelines for a memorable visit.

GPS Coordinates: 35.2658° N, 112.0572° W

Best Time to Visit: Spring - Summer

Pass/Permit/fees: The tickets cost $9-$15. Kids under 2 are free.

Did you Know? It offers nature and wildlife enthusiasts.

Winslow

1. Meteor Crater & Barringer Space Museum

Meteor Crater, or Barringer Crater, is a remarkable natural wonder near Winslow, Arizona. With a diameter of about 1.2 kilometers and a depth of 170 meters, it is the best-preserved impact crater on Earth. Visitors to the Meteor Crater can witness the immense power of a meteorite's impact and explore the interactive museum showcasing the crater's history, geology, and scientific significance. The Barringer Space Museum offers a wealth of information about space exploration, meteorites, and the universe, making it an educational and fascinating destination for astronomy enthusiasts of all ages.

Location: Arizona 86047, USA

Closest City or Town: Show Low, AZ.

How to Get There: To reach Meteor Crater and the Barringer Space Museum, travel to Winslow, Arizona, about 35 miles east of Flagstaff on Interstate 40.

GPS Coordinates: 35°01'41"N, 111°01'24"W

Best Time to Visit: Summer

Pass/Permit/fees: The tickets cost $18-$27. Kids under 13 are free.

Did you Know? It is famous for Space Museum educational exhibits, delving into space exploration, and meteorites.

Petrified Forest National Park

1. Petrified Forest National Park

Petrified Forest National Park, located in northeastern Arizona, is a geological wonder that offers a mesmerizing journey into the ancient past. The park spans over 200 square miles and is renowned for its stunning displays of petrified wood, fossils, and vibrant badlands. Visitors can explore many trails, revealing magnificent petrified logs that have transformed into lively, colorful stones over millions of years. Additionally, the park is home to fascinating archaeological sites and exhibits that shed light on the rich cultural history of the region's indigenous people. Petrified Forest National Park is a captivating destination that showcases the beauty and wonders of nature's transformative power.

Location: Arizona, USA

Closest City or Town: Flagstaff, AZ.

How to Get There: To reach Petrified Forest National Park, travel to northeastern Arizona through either the north entrance near Holbrook or the south entrance near Chambers.

GPS Coordinates: 35.0037° N, 109.7889° W

Best Time to Visit: September-December

Pass/Permit/fees: The tickets cost $5-$10.

Did you Know? Visitors can explore the park's stunning landscapes and hike the designated trails.

2. Painted Desert

The Painted Desert, a breathtaking natural wonder, stretches across northern Arizona and is part of the larger Petrified Forest National Park. This mesmerizing landscape is a vivid display of vibrant colors, with layers of sedimentary rock revealing red, orange, purple, and pink hues. As sunlight dances upon the desert, it creates a magical panorama that captivates the senses. Visitors can explore the Painted Desert through scenic drives, overlooks, and hiking trails, allowing for an immersive experience in this otherworldly expanse. The Painted Desert is a testament to the Earth's artistry, offering a glimpse into the wonders of geological evolution.

Location: Northeastern Arizona

Closest City or Town: Sedona, AZ.

How to Get There: Travel to northeastern Arizona and enter Petrified Forest National Park through either the north entrance near Holbrook or the south entrance near Chambers.

GPS Coordinates: 35.5003° N, 110.0840° W

Best Time to Visit: Spring

Pass/Permit/fees: The tickets cost $20.

Did you Know? Visitors can enjoy scenic drives
and hiking trails within the park?

HUALAPAI

1.   Grand Canyon Skywalk

The Grand Canyon Skywalk is an awe-inspiring architectural marvel located in the western part of the Grand Canyon in Arizona. This horseshoe-shaped glass bridge extends about 70 feet from the canyon's rim, allowing visitors to walk above the vast chasm with a transparent view of the canyon floor nearly a mile below. It offers a thrilling and unforgettable experience, providing panoramic views of the breathtaking landscape. With its engineering excellence and natural beauty, the Grand Canyon Skywalk provides a unique opportunity to feel the grandeur and immensity of one of the world's most iconic natural wonders.

Location: Peach Springs, AZ 86434, USA

Closest City or Town: Kingman, AZ.

How to Get There: To reach the Grand Canyon Skywalk:

Travel to Peach Springs, Arizona, on the Hualapai Indian Reservation.

GPS Coordinates: 36.0119° N, 113.8108° W

Best Time to Visit: Fall

Pass/Permit/fees: The tickets cost $19-$45.

Did you Know? You can enjoy the thrilling experience of walking on the glass bridge with breathtaking views of the Grand Canyon?

OATMAN

1. Sitgreaves Pass

Sitgreaves Pass is a scenic mountain pass in the Black Mountains of northwestern Arizona near Oatman. Rising to an elevation of approximately 3,550 feet, it offers a thrilling and picturesque drive through the rugged desert terrain. The pass showcases breathtaking views of the surrounding valleys, canyons, and towering rock formations. With its winding roads and steep gradients, Sitgreaves Pass provides a memorable journey for adventurers and nature lovers alike. Whether driving through or stopping to admire the stunning vistas, Sitgreaves Pass promises a captivating experience in the heart of Arizona's stunning landscapes.

Location: Oatman Rd, Golden Valley, AZ

Closest City or Town: Bullhead City, AZ.

How to Get There: To reach Sitgreaves Pass, drive along Historic Route 66 between Oatman and Kingman in northwest Arizona.

Enjoy the scenic drive as you navigate the winding roads and steep gradients, taking in the breathtaking views of the surrounding desert landscapes.

GPS Coordinates: 35.0458° N, 114.3605° W

Best Time to Visit: Fall

Pass/Permit/fees: You can book a ticket online.

Did you Know? You can enjoy a safe and memorable journey through Sitgreaves Pass?

CHINLE

1. Spider Rock

Spider Rock is a mesmerizing natural formation in Canyon de Chelly National Monument, Arizona. A stunning sandstone spire is an iconic symbol of Navajo legend and spirituality. The rock's vertical walls and intricate texture create a captivating sight, especially during sunrise and sunset when the sunlight bathes it in a golden glow. Spider Rock holds deep cultural significance for the Navajo people, who believe it is home to Spider Woman, a powerful and protective deity. Visiting Spider Rock profoundly connects to the region's rich history and spiritual beliefs.

Location: Hwy Rte 7, Chinle, AZ 86503, United States

Closest City or Town: Ganado, AZ.

How to Get There: To reach Spider Rock in Canyon de Chelly National Monument.Travel to Chinle, Arizona, the closest town to the monument.

GPS Coordinates: 36.1083° N, 109.3507° W

Best Time to Visit: Summer

Pass/Permit/fees: The tickets cost $7.

Did you Know? You can explore the majestic beauty and cultural significance of Spider Rock?

2. Canyon de Chelly National Monument

Canyon de Chelly National Monument in northeastern Arizona is a remarkable testament to natural beauty and rich cultural history. Carved by the relentless force of the water over millions of years, the deep canyons of Canyon de Chelly offer breathtaking vistas of towering cliffs, hidden nooks, and vibrant desert landscapes. The monument is also home to ancient ruins, petroglyphs, and pictographs that tell the story of the ancestral Puebloans who once inhabited the area. Visitors can explore the canyons through guided tours, hike along designated trails, and immerse themselves in this sacred place's deep connection between nature and human heritage.

Location: Chinle, AZ, USA

Closest City or Town: Winslow, AZ.

How to Get There: To visit Canyon de Chelly National Monument:

1.Travel to Chinle, Arizona, the nearest town.

2.From there, drive to the visitor center to pay the entrance fee and obtain information about the park.

GPS Coordinates: 36.1191° N, 109.3197° W

Best Time to Visit: Summer, Winter

Pass/Permit/fees: Entry is free.

Did you Know? You can explore the national monument's captivating beauty and rich cultural history?

GRAND CANYON NATIONAL PARK

1. Grand Canyon National Park

Grand Canyon National Park is a breathtaking marvel in the southwestern United States. Spanning over 1.2 million acres in Arizona, it is renowned for its awe-inspiring beauty and geological significance. The park is dominated by the iconic Grand Canyon, a massive gorge carved by the Colorado River over millions of years. The sheer magnitude and intricate rock formations make it a natural wonder of the world. The park offers many activities, including hiking, rafting, and camping, providing visitors with unforgettable experiences. Beyond its stunning vistas, the Grand Canyon National Park is a sanctuary for diverse wildlife and a testament to the Earth's captivating history.

Location: Arizona, USA

Closest City or Town: Flagstaff, AZ.

How to Get There: To reach Grand Canyon National Park, fly to Phoenix Sky Harbor International Airport and drive approximately 3.5 hours to the South Rim. Alternatively, take the Grand Canyon Railway from Williams, Arizona, for a scenic train journey.

GPS Coordinates: 36.2679° N, 112.3535° W

Best Time to Visit: March-May

Pass/Permit/fees: The ticket costs $20.

Did you Know? It is known for breathtaking views and hiking the rim trails?

2. Grand Canyon South Rim

The Grand Canyon South Rim is a breathtaking natural wonder in northern Arizona, USA. Spanning approximately 277 miles long and up to 18 miles wide, it offers a mesmerizing display of geological formations and vibrant colors. The South Rim, being the most accessible and popular part of the Grand Canyon, attracts millions of visitors each year. From its numerous viewpoints, such as Mather Point and Yavapai Observation Station, visitors can marvel at the vastness and beauty of the canyon, with its towering cliffs and deep gorges carved by the Colorado River. Hiking trails, including the renowned Bright Angel Trail, provide opportunities for exploration and unforgettable experiences amidst this awe-inspiring landscape.

Location: Grand Canyon Village, AZ 86023, United States

Closest City or Town: Tusayan, AZ.

How to Get There: The Grand Canyon South Rim beckons with its majestic beauty, accessible by car, shuttle bus, or train. From nearby cities or airports, embark on a journey to witness the awe-inspiring vistas and explore the numerous viewpoints and hiking trails that await

GPS Coordinates: 36.0604° N, 112.1076° W

Best Time to Visit: April-June

Pass/Permit/fees: The ticket costs $35

Did you Know? It is a must-visit destination for all nature enthusiasts?

3.   Grand Canyon North Rim

The Grand Canyon North Rim offers a more secluded and serene experience than its bustling South Rim counterpart. It is located in a remote part of Arizona and boasts stunning vistas and a cooler, alpine environment. The North Rim is known for its unique rock formations, including the iconic Cape Royal and Point Imperial. Visitors can take in panoramic views from various viewpoints and enjoy hiking trails that meander through forests of pine and aspen trees. With fewer crowds and a tranquil ambiance, the Grand Canyon North Rim provides a peaceful retreat and an opportunity to immerse oneself in the wonders of nature.

Location: North Rim Arizona 86052, USA

Closest City or Town: Tusayan, AZ.

How to Get There: To reach the Grand Canyon North Rim, drive through scenic routes or take a shuttle bus from the South Rim during the summer. Alternatively, fly to St. George Regional Airport and rent a car for a picturesque drive.

GPS Coordinates: 36.2135° N, 112.0581° W

Best Time to Visit: March-May

Pass/Permit/fees: The ticket costs $35.

Did you Know? It is famous for its breathtaking views and hiking trails?

4.   Grand Canyon Desert View Watchtower

The Desert View Watchtower is a magnetic structure on the South Rim of the Grand Canyon, Arizona. Architect Mary Colter's design uniquely blends Native American, and Art Deco influences. The watchtower provides visitors with panoramic views of the surrounding canyon and the Colorado River. Inside, you can explore the multi-level structure, climb the observation deck, and admire the stunning murals depicting Native American culture. The Desert View Watchtower is a testament to the rich history and architectural marvels within the Grand Canyon, providing a memorable experience for all who visit.

Location: Desert View Watchtower, Grand Canyon Village, AZ 86023, USA

Closest City or Town: Jacob Lake, AZ.

How to Get There: To reach the Grand Canyon Desert View Watchtower, drive along Highway 64 from the Grand Canyon Village on the South Rim, following signs to the Desert View area. Alternatively, take the free Orange Route shuttle bus from the village.

GPS Coordinates: 36.0441° N, 111.8262° W

Best Time to Visit: April-September

Pass/Permit/fees: Different packages are available.

Did you Know?   You can explore stunning views here?

5.   Bright Angel Point

Bright Angel Point is a stunning viewpoint on the North Rim of the Grand Canyon, Arizona. It offers breathtaking panoramic vistas and is a popular destination for visitors seeking a remarkable vantage point. Accessible via a short, scenic trail, the end provides awe-inspiring views of the vast canyon, its colorful rock formations, and the winding Colorado River below. The experience of standing at Bright Angel Point evokes a sense of wonder and awe, allowing visitors to appreciate the grandeur and immensity of nature's masterpiece. It is a must-visit destination for those seeking a memorable encounter with the majesty of the Grand Canyon.

Location: Bright Angel Point Trail, North Rim, AZ 86052, United States

Closest City or Town: Seligman, AZ.

How to Get There: To reach Bright Angel Point on the Grand Canyon's North Rim, drive along Highway 67 from the North Rim Entrance Station, following signs to the Grand Canyon Lodge. A short walk along a paved trail will lead you to the viewpoint.

GPS Coordinates: 36.1935° N, 112.0486° W

Best Time to Visit: Spring, Fall

Pass/Permit/fees: The ticket costs $15.

Did you Know? You can enjoy awe-inspiring views?

6. Hopi Point

Hopi Point is a stunning viewpoint on the South Rim of the Grand Canyon, Arizona. Known for its unparalleled panoramic vistas, it is a popular destination for visitors seeking a breathtaking experience. Accessible by car or shuttle bus, Hopi Point offers a dramatic overlook of the vast canyon, showcasing its towering cliffs, intricate rock formations, and the meandering Colorado River below. With its expansive vistas and stunning sunsets, Hopi Point provides a mesmerizing setting for photographers and nature enthusiasts alike,

allowing them to witness the timeless beauty and grandeur of the Grand Canyon in all its splendor.

Location: Hopi Point Arizona 86023, United States

Closest City or Town: Meadview, AZ.

How to Get There: To reach Hopi Point on the Grand Canyon's South Rim, drive along Desert View Drive (Highway 64) from the Grand Canyon Village, following the signs to the viewpoint.

GPS Coordinates: 36.0744° N, 112.1550° W

Best Time to Visit: Spring, Fall

Pass/Permit/fees: The ticket costs $15.

Did you Know? You can enjoy the majestic view here?

7. Grandview Point

Grandview Point is a stunning viewpoint on the South Rim of the Grand Canyon, Arizona. Known for its spectacular panoramic views, it offers a glimpse into the awe-inspiring beauty of the canyon. Accessible by car or shuttle bus, Grandview Point showcases the sheer magnitude of the Grand Canyon with its vast cliffs, colorful rock formations, and the winding Colorado River below. The point also holds historical significance, as it was once a mining site in the early 20th century. Standing at Grandview Point, visitors can immerse themselves in the grandeur of nature and witness the timeless splendor of the Grand Canyon.

Location: Grandview Pt Arizona 86023, USA

Closest City or Town: Peach Springs, AZ.

How to Get There: To reach Grandview Point on the Grand Canyon's South Rim, drive along Desert View Drive (Highway 64) from the

Grand Canyon Village, following the signs to the viewpoint. Alternatively, take the free Orange Route shuttle from the village to Grandview Point.

GPS Coordinates: 35.9985° N, 111.9878° W

Best Time to Visit: March-May

Pass/Permit/fees: Entry is free.

Did you Know? It is famous for expansive views of towering cliffs and the meandering Colorado River below?

8.   Historic Navajo Bridge

The Historic Navajo Bridge is a fascinating landmark near Marble Canyon in northern Arizona, USA. Built-in 1929, it was a crucial crossing point over the Colorado River, connecting Arizona's north and southern regions. This architectural marvel stands as a testament to human engineering and innovation. Today, the old bridge has been replaced by a newer structure, but the Historic Navajo Bridge remains a reminder of the past. It attracts visitors with its unique design and offers breathtaking views of the river and the surrounding scenic landscape, making it a must-visit destination for history enthusiasts and nature lovers alike.

Location: US-89A, Marble Canyon, AZ 86036, USA

Closest City or Town: Marble Canyon, AZ.

How to Get There: To reach the Historic Navajo Bridge near Marble Canyon in Arizona, drive east on Highway 89A from the South Rim of the Grand Canyon. Follow the signs for Navajo Bridge.

GPS Coordinates: 36.8176° N, 111.6312° W

Best Time to Visit: Summer

Pass/Permit/fees: Entry is free.

Did you Know? You can enjoy the Colorado River's scenic views and appreciate this iconic landmark's historical significance?

9.   Lipan Point

Lipan Point is a stunning viewpoint located on the South Rim of the Grand Canyon in Arizona. Offering breathtaking panoramic vistas, it is a popular destination for visitors seeking a remarkable experience. Accessible by car or shuttle bus, Lipan Point provides a dramatic overlook of the expansive canyon, revealing its awe-inspiring depths, towering cliffs, and the meandering Colorado River below. With its unobstructed views and stunning sunsets, Lipan Point offers a lovely setting for photographers and nature enthusiasts alike, allowing them to witness the timeless beauty and grandeur of the Grand Canyon in all its glory.

Location: Grand Canyon Village, AZ 86023, United States

Closest City or Town: Marble Canyon, AZ.

How to Get There: To reach Lipan Point on the Grand Canyon's South Rim, drive along Desert View Drive (Highway 64) from the Grand Canyon Village, following signs to the viewpoint. Alternatively, take the free Orange Route shuttle from the village to Lipan Point.

GPS Coordinates: 36.0330° N, 111.8532° W

Best Time to Visit: Spring

Pass/Permit/fees: Different packages are available.

Did you Know? It is famous for its beauty.

10.   Bright Angel Trail

Bright Angel Trail is a renowned hiking trail in Arizona's Grand Canyon National Park. This iconic trail is known for its breathtaking beauty and challenging terrain, offering hikers a chance to explore the depths of the Grand Canyon. Spanning about 9.5 miles from the South Rim to the Colorado River, it presents a variety of stunning viewpoints and geological features along the way. Hikers can witness the magnificent layers of rock formations, encounter diverse flora and fauna, and experience the thrill of descending into the heart of the canyon. Bright Angel Trail is a must-do adventure for outdoor enthusiasts seeking an unforgettable Grand Canyon experience.

Location: Grand Canyon National Park, Arizona, United States

Closest City or Town: Sedona, AZ.

How to Get There: To access Bright Angel Trail in Arizona's Grand Canyon National Park, drive to the Grand Canyon Village and follow signs to the trailhead. Alternatively, take the Blue Route shuttle bus to the Bright Angel Lodge, where you can easily walk to the trailhead.

GPS Coordinates: 36.0575° N, 112.1392° W

Best Time to Visit: Spring

Pass/Permit/fees: Different packages are available.

Did you Know? You can explore the beauty and diverse landscapes?

11.   South Kaibab Trail

The South Kaibab Trail is a spectacular hiking route in Arizona's Grand Canyon National Park. Known for its stunning vistas and challenging terrain, it offers a thrilling adventure for outdoor enthusiasts. Starting near Yaki Point, the trail descends steeply into the canyon, showcasing breathtaking panoramic views.

Hikers can marvel at the vivid rock layers and the immense scale of the Grand Canyon. With limited shade and water, being well-prepared and bringing plenty of supplies is crucial. The South Kaibab Trail provides a memorable experience, rewarding hikers with unforgettable scenery and a deeper connection to this natural wonder.

Location: S Kaibab Trail Arizona, USA

Closest City or Town: Peach Springs, AZ.

How to Get There: To access the South Kaibab Trail in Arizona's Grand Canyon National Park, drive east on Desert View Drive (Highway 64) from the Grand Canyon Village, following signs to the trailhead. Alternatively, take the free Orange Route shuttle bus to Yaki Point, the starting point of the South Kaibab Trail.

GPS Coordinates: 36.0529° N, 112.0830.° W

Best Time to Visit: Spring

Pass/Permit/fees: Different packages are available.

Did you Know? It is famous for hiking.

12.   Mather Point

Mather Point is a breathtaking viewpoint on the South Rim of the Grand Canyon in Arizona, USA. Named after Stephen Mather, the first director of the National Park Service, it offers an awe-inspiring panorama of the majestic canyon. Standing at Mather Point, visitors are treated to an expansive vista that showcases the geological wonders of the Grand Canyon, with its intricate layers of red, orange, and brown rocks carved by the mighty Colorado River over millions of years. The site is genuinely awe-inspiring, evoking a sense of wonder and reverence for the natural world. Mather Point is a must-visit destination for nature enthusiasts and adventure seekers, providing a glimpse into the grandeur of one of the world's most iconic natural landmarks.

Location: Rim Trail, Grand Canyon Village, AZ 86023, USA

Closest City or Town: Peach Springs, AZ.

How to Get There: To get to Mather Point at Grand Canyon National Park:

1.Drive or take a shuttle bus to the South Rim Visitor Center.

2.Follow signs or ask for directions to Mather Point.

GPS Coordinates: 36.0617° N, 112.1077° W

Best Time to Visit: Spring, Summer

Pass/Permit/fees: The ticket costs $15.

Did you Know? You can enjoy stunning panoramic views of the Grand Canyon?

13. Hermit's Rest

Hermit's Rest is a historic landmark and scenic viewpoint located on the South Rim of the Grand Canyon in Arizona. Designed by renowned architect Mary Colter, this rustic stone structure is a picturesque stop along the Hermit Road, offering visitors stunning panoramic canyon views. Its unique architecture blends harmoniously with the natural surroundings, and the cozy interior invites visitors to relax and appreciate the canyon's grandeur. Whether enjoying the breathtaking sunset views, hiking along nearby trails, or learning about the area's history and geology, Hermit's Rest is a must-visit destination for those seeking an unforgettable experience at the Grand Canyon.

Location: Grand Canyon Village, AZ 86023, USA

Closest City or Town: Peach Springs, AZ.

How to Get There: To get to Hermit's Rest, located on the South Rim of the Grand Canyon in Arizona, visitors can take the free shuttle bus known as the Hermit Road Route from the Grand Canyon Village.

GPS Coordinates: 36.0621° N, 112.2112° W

Best Time to Visit: Spring, Summer

Pass/Permit/fees: The ticket costs $135.

Did you Know? It is famous for its historical architecture.

SUPAI

1. Havasu Falls

Havasu Falls is a breathtaking natural wonder located within the Havasupai Indian Reservation in Arizona. Its crystal-clear turquoise waters cascading down vibrant red rocks make it a paradise for nature lovers. The falls and nearby waterfalls, such as Mooney Falls and Beaver Falls, create a series of stunning cascades in a remote and pristine canyon. Accessible only by a challenging hike or helicopter, the journey to Havasu Falls is well worth the effort. Visitors can swim in the deep blue pools, camp in the campground, and immerse themselves in the awe-inspiring beauty of this hidden gem in the desert.

Location: Havasu Falls, Arizona 86435, USA

Closest City or Town: Chino Valley, AZ.

How to Get There: 1. Make a reservation with the Havasupai Tribe.

1.Travel to Hualapai Hilltop and hike 10 miles to Supai Village.

GPS Coordinates: 36.2552° N, 112.6979° W

Best Time to Visit: Spring, Summer, early winter

Pass/Permit/fees: The ticket costs $100.

Did you Know? It is famous for the breathtaking beauty of the falls and surrounding pools?

ARIZONA BUCKET LIST

PAGE

1. Glen Canyon National Recreation Area

Glen Canyon National Recreation Area, situated in Utah and Arizona, is a stunning landscape encompassing a vast desert, canyons, and the iconic Lake Powell. Its dramatic red rock cliffs, deep canyons, and shimmering blue waters offer a haven for outdoor enthusiasts. Visitors can partake in many activities, such as boating, fishing, hiking, camping, and exploring the hidden slot canyons. The area also houses historical sites like the Rainbow Bridge National Monument, the largest natural bridge in the world. Glen Canyon National Recreation Area is a captivating destination showcasing the Southwest's raw beauty.

Location: 691 Scenic View Rd Dr, Page, AZ 86040, USA

Closest City or Town: Hurricane, UT

How to Get There: To get to Glen Canyon National Recreation Area:

1- Determine your destination within the area.

2- Plan your transportation by car or air, and follow directions.

GPS Coordinates: 37.3867° N, 110.8424° W

Best Time to Visit: March-December

Pass/Permit/fees: Different packages are available.

Did you Know? It is famous for outdoor activities such as boating, hiking, and exploring the breathtaking canyons.

2. Antelope Canyon

Antelope Canyon near Page, Arizona, is a mesmerizing slot canyon renowned for its ethereal beauty and stunning light beams. Carved by years of natural erosion, the canyon's narrow sandstone walls showcase mesmerizing patterns, curves, and textures. Its iconic orange and red hues offer visitors a photographer's paradise and a spiritual experience. Guided tours are available to explore the Upper Antelope Canyon and Lower Antelope Canyon, allowing visitors to witness the interplay of light and shadow as sunlight streams through the narrow openings above. Antelope Canyon is a captivating natural wonder that leaves visitors in awe of its otherworldly charm.

Location: 22 S Lake Powell Blvd, Page, AZ 86040, USA

Closest City or Town: Cedar City, UT

How to Get There: To get to Antelope Canyon:

1. Plan your trip and make reservations for a guided tour in advance.

2. Travel to Page, Arizona, by car or flying into nearby airports.

GPS Coordinates: 36.9180° N, 111.4595° W

103

Best Time to Visit: March-October

Pass/Permit/fees: The ticket costs $100.

Did you Know? You can explore the breathtaking beauty of Antelope Canyon?

3. Vermilion Cliffs National Monument

Vermilion Cliffs National Monument, located in northern Arizona, is a mesmerizing and diverse landscape showcasing the raw beauty of the Southwest's desert. Spanning over 280,000 acres, it is a treasure trove of geological wonders, including the famous Wave Formation, Coyote Buttes, and the striking Vermilion Cliffs. The monument's vibrant sandstone cliffs, deep canyons, and unique rock formations create a dramatic backdrop for outdoor enthusiasts and photographers alike. Hiking, backpacking, and wildlife viewing opportunities abound, offering a chance to witness the rare California condor and other desert wildlife. Vermilion Cliffs National Monument is a captivating destination showcasing the Arizona desert's untamed spirit.

Location: Marble Canyon, AZ 86036, USA

Closest City or Town: Cedar City, UT

How to Get There: To get to Vermilion Cliffs National Monument:

1- Plan your visit and research the specific area or attraction you want to explore.

2- Depending on your destination, either drive or hike to the entry points and trailheads within the monument.

GPS Coordinates: 36.8625° N, 111.8270° W

Best Time to Visit: April-October

Pass/Permit/fees: The ticket costs $10.

Did you Know? It is famous for its awe-inspiring landscapes?

4. Horseshoe Bend

Horseshoe Bend is a remarkable natural wonder located near Page, Arizona. Carved by the mighty Colorado River, it presents a stunning horseshoe-shaped curve in the canyon. At the edge of the 1,000-foot cliffs, visitors are treated to breathtaking panoramic views of the meandering river below and the surrounding red sandstone cliffs. The combination of the deep blue water, the contrasting red rocks, and the vastness of the landscape create a truly awe-inspiring sight. Horseshoe Bend has become a popular tourist destination, attracting nature lovers and photographers from around the world. It is a testament to the beauty and power of nature's geological wonders.

Location: 1001 Page Parkway, Page, AZ 86040, USA

Closest City or Town: Washington, UT

How to Get There: To reach Horseshoe Bend:

1.Travel to Page, Arizona.

2.Drive south on Highway 89 and follow the signs to the well-marked parking area.

3.Take a short hike along the trail to reach the overlook.

GPS Coordinates: 36.8791° N, 111.5104° W

Best Time to Visit: Fall

Pass/Permit/fees: Entry is free.

Did you Know? You can enjoy the stunning views of the horseshoe-shaped bend carved by the Colorado River?

5. Glen Canyon Dam Overlook

ARIZONA BUCKET LIST

The Glen Canyon Dam Overlook is a breathtaking destination that offers a mesmerizing view of one of America's engineering marvels. This scenic viewpoint in Arizona provides a panoramic vista of the mighty Glen Canyon Dam. With its imposing structure and the tranquil waters of the Colorado River snaking through the magnificent red rock canyons, the scene is nothing short of awe-inspiring. Visitors can marvel at the immense scale of the dam, which stands as a testament to human ingenuity and the quest for harnessing natural resources. The Glen Canyon Dam Overlook is a must-visit for nature enthusiasts, photographers, and anyone seeking to witness the grandeur of nature and human accomplishment in perfect harmony.

Location: Glen Canyon Dam Overlook Page, AZ 86040, USA

Closest City or Town: Flagstaff, AZ

How to Get There: To reach the Glen Canyon Dam Overlook, travel to Page, Arizona. From the Carl Hayden Visitor Center, follow signs or ask for directions.

GPS Coordinates: 36.9244° N, 111.4784° W

Best Time to Visit: Summer

Pass/Permit/fees: The ticket costs $30.

Did you Know? You can explore the grandeur of the dam and its breathtaking surroundings?

6. White Pockets

White Pocket is a mesmerizing natural wonder near the Vermilion Cliffs National Monument in northern Arizona. This unique geological formation is a hidden gem characterized by its swirling white and red sandstone formations that resemble a surreal, otherworldly landscape. The intricate patterns and shapes carved by wind and water over millions of years create a captivating visual spectacle. White Pocket offers photographers and outdoor enthusiasts a playground with striking formations, vibrant colors, and diverse textures. Accessible via a challenging off-road journey, this remote destination provides an opportunity for solitude and an immersive connection with nature. Exploring White Pocket is like stepping into a dreamscape, where the beauty of the Earth's natural artistry is fully displayed.

Location: House Rock Valley Road (BLM 1065)

Closest City or Town: Flagstaff, AZ

How to Get There: White Pocket, located in northern Arizona, is a remote and mesmerizing natural wonder characterized by its swirling white and red sandstone formations. Accessible only by a challenging off-road journey, this hidden gem offers a surreal and otherworldly landscape that captivates visitors.

GPS Coordinates: 36.9561° N, 111.9043° W

Best Time to Visit: Summer

Pass/Permit/fees: The ticket costs $25.

Did you Know? You can explore awe-inspiring beauty in the Earth's natural artistry?

TUBA CITY

2.Plan your trip and follow safety guidelines.

GPS Coordinates: 36.1029° N, 111.3176° W

Best Time to Visit: Summer, Fall

Pass/Permit/fees: Entry is free.

Did you Know? Explore designated paths, observe the tracks, and engage with experts if available?

1. Dinosaur Tracks

Dinosaur tracks are fossilized imprints left behind by ancient creatures, offering a glimpse into the prehistoric world. These remarkable footprints provide evidence of the existence and behavior of dinosaurs that roamed the Earth millions of years ago. Preserved in various locations worldwide, such as national parks and museums, dinosaur tracks are a captivating sight for scientists and enthusiasts. They connect to our planet's distant past, sparking wonder and curiosity about these magnificent creatures. Exploring these tracks allows us to imagine the colossal footsteps and the ancient ecosystems where dinosaurs thrived once.

Location: Dinosaur Tracks Arizona 86045, USA

Closest City or Town: Winslow, AZ

How to Get There: To view dinosaur tracks:

1.Research locations known for tracks.

MONUMENT VALLEY

1. Monument Valley Navajo Tribal Park

Monument Valley Navajo Tribal Park is a captivating destination that showcases the iconic red sandstone buttes and mesas, immortalized in countless Western movies and photographs. Located on the Navajo Nation reservation, this majestic park offers visitors a glimpse into the rich Native American culture and breathtaking natural beauty. The towering rock formations, dramatic cliffs, and vast desert landscapes create a surreal and awe-inspiring setting. Exploring the park's scenic drives, hiking trails, and guided tours allows visitors to immerse themselves in this sacred land's timeless beauty and spiritual significance. Monument Valley Navajo Tribal Park is a must-visit for those seeking a truly unforgettable experience in the heart of the American Southwest.

Location: U.S. 163 Scenic, Oljato-Monument Valley, AZ 84536, USA

Closest City or Town: Flagstaff, AZ

How to Get There: To get to Monument Valley Navajo Tribal Park:

1. Plan your trip to the Arizona-Utah border.

2. Drive to Kayenta, Arizona, and take U.S. Highway 163 north.

3. Follow signs to the park entrance and pay the entrance fee at the visitor center.

GPS Coordinates: 36.9669° N, 110.0796° W

Best Time to Visit: Fall

Pass/Permit/fees: The ticket costs $8.

Did you Know? It is famous for its uniqueness?

PAYSON

1. Tonto Natural Bridge State Park

Tonto Natural Bridge State Park, nestled in the heart of Arizona, is a natural wonder that showcases the world's largest natural travertine bridge. This stunning formation, sculpted over millions of years by the forces of nature, creates a mesmerizing sight. Visitors can explore the park's trails and witness the majestic bridge up close, marveling at its intricate beauty. The park offers breathtaking views, tranquil picnic areas, and birdwatching and wildlife spotting opportunities. Tonto Natural Bridge State Park is a haven for nature lovers, providing a unique and unforgettable experience amid Arizona's rugged landscapes.

Location: Nf-583A, Pine, AZ 85544, USA

Closest City or Town: Camp Verde, AZ

How to Get There: To get to Tonto Natural Bridge State Park:

1.Plan your trip to Payson, Arizona.

2.Take State Route 87 North and follow signs to the park entrance.

GPS Coordinates: 34.3229° N, 111.4544° W

Best Time to Visit: Fall, Spring

Pass/Permit/fees: The ticket costs $7. Kids under 6 are free.

Did you Know? It is famous for its magnificent natural bridge.

ARIZONA BUCKET LIST

PLANNING

Introduction

Arizona has diverse landscapes and captivating destinations with unique charm and allure. From the awe-inspiring Grand Canyon to the vibrant city of Phoenix, this southwestern state offers many experiences for travelers. We have divided the 150 notable locations into 14 distinct zones to navigate the abundance of destinations. Each zone encompasses a group of cities and towns that share geographical proximity and similar attractions. In this chapter, we will explore the highlights of each site, delving into the nearby villages and their fascinating features. From the scenic wonders of the desert to the cultural treasures tucked away in historic towns, join us on a journey through Arizona's zones as we uncover the hidden gems and renowned destinations that make this state a captivating and diverse travel destination.

First Zone

Phoenix, Glendale, Scottsdale, Mesa, Gilbert, Chandler, Apache Junction, Tortilla Flat, Coolidge, Picacho, Wickenburg, and Superior are located in Arizona's greater Phoenix metropolitan area. This region, often called the "Valley of the Sun," is a bustling and vibrant hub known for its warm climate, stunning desert landscapes, and many attractions and activities.

Phoenix is Arizona's capital and largest city, offering a dynamic urban environment with cultural institutions like the Heard Museum and Phoenix Art Museum, professional sports teams, and a thriving dining and entertainment scene. Nearby, Glendale is renowned for its sports venues, including State Farm Stadium and Gila River Arena, while Scottsdale is famous for its upscale resorts, golf courses, and vibrant nightlife. Mesa, Gilbert, and Chandler are suburban cities known for their family-friendly neighborhoods, excellent schools, and diverse recreational opportunities, including parks, hiking trails, and golf courses. Apache Junction is near the Superstition Mountains and is a gateway to outdoor adventures like hiking, camping, and exploring the nearby Tonto National Forest.

Tortilla Flat is a charming small community nestled in the Superstition Mountains, offering a taste of Old West ambiance with its historic buildings and Western-style saloons. Coolidge, Picacho, Wickenburg, and Superior are smaller towns in the region, each with unique charm and attractions.

Overall, the first zone comprising these cities in the Phoenix metropolitan area provides diverse experiences, from vibrant urban life to tranquil desert retreats, making it an enticing destination for residents and visitors alike.

1.Phoenix

2.Glendale

3.Scottsdale

4.Mesa

5.Gilbert

6.Chandler

7.Apache Junction

8.Tortilla Flat

9.Coolidge

10.Picacho

11.Wickenburg

12.Superior

Second Zone

The cities of Tucson, Mount Lemmon, Vail, Sahuarita, Benson, Tombstone, Willcox, and Bisbee are part of the second zone in southern Arizona. This region is known for its stunning natural landscapes, rich history, and unique cultural attractions.

Tucson, the largest city in southern Arizona, offers a vibrant mix of desert beauty and urban amenities. It is home to the University of Arizona, bringing youthful energy to the city. Visitors can explore the historic downtown area, visit the Arizona-Sonora Desert Museum, or hike in the beautiful Saguaro National Park. Mount Lemmon is a popular getaway located in the Santa Catalina Mountains. As the highest point in the region, it provides an excellent escape during the summer months and offers scenic drives, hiking trails, and ski slopes in the winter.

Vail and Sahuarita are suburban communities located just outside of Tucson, known for their peaceful surroundings and access to outdoor activities such as hiking and birdwatching. Benson is a gateway to the beautiful Dragoon Mountains and the Kartchner Caverns State Park, which boasts stunning underground formations. Tombstone is a historic town famous for its Wild West heritage and the legendary gunfight at the O.K. Corral. Visitors can revisit and experience the Old West through reenactments and historical tours. Willcox is a charming small town renowned for its vineyards and wineries, allowing wine enthusiasts to sample local varietals. Bisbee is a picturesque town in the Mule Mountains, known for its colorful architecture, art galleries, and mining history.

The second zone in southern Arizona provides a mix of natural beauty, historical sites, and cultural experiences, making it a captivating destination for those seeking adventure, relaxation, and a taste of the Old West.

1.Tucson

2.Mount Lemmon

3.Vail

4.Sahuarita

5.Benson

6.Tombstone

7.Willcox

8.Bisbee

Third Zone

Ajo is a small desert town in southern Arizona, surrounded by awe-inspiring landscapes and a rich historical legacy. With its roots deeply intertwined with copper mining, Ajo's history is reflected in its unique architecture and the echoes of the mining industry that once thrived there. The town's Spanish-style buildings and the vibrant Ajo Plaza are a testament to its cultural heritage. Ajo's natural beauty is equally captivating, with rugged mountains and a diverse desert ecosystem beckoning outdoor enthusiasts to explore its trails and indulge in activities like birdwatching or stargazing. The town's welcoming community spirit is palpable, evident in its vibrant arts scene, regular community events, and the strong camaraderie permeating every corner of Ajo.

1.Ajo

Fourth Zone

Yuma, located in the southwestern corner of Arizona, is steeped in rich history and surrounded by breathtaking natural beauty. Situated along the banks of the Colorado River, Yuma has served as a significant crossing point and a hub of activity throughout the centuries. The city's historical sites, such as the Yuma Territorial Prison State Historic Park and the Yuma Quartermaster Depot State Historical Park, offer a glimpse into its storied past. Beyond its historical charm, Yuma boasts a vibrant cultural scene, with festivals and events that celebrate the region's diverse heritage. Outdoor enthusiasts will find plenty to explore, from boating and fishing on the Colorado River to hiking through nearby desert trails. Yuma's agritourism scene also invites visitors to discover the region's agricultural prowess as they partake in farm tours and indulge in the freshest local produce. With its captivating blend of history, culture, and natural beauty, Yuma is an enticing destination for travelers seeking a unique and enriching experience.

1.Yuma

Fifth Zone

The fifth zone in Arizona consists of the cities of Camp Verde, Rimrock, Cottonwood, Clarkdale, Jerome, Village of Oak Creek, and Sedona. This region is nestled amidst the stunning landscapes of central Arizona and offers a unique blend of natural beauty, rich history, and artistic charm.

Camp Verde is a small town that serves as a gateway to the Verde Valley and offers opportunities for outdoor recreation, including hiking, camping, and exploring the scenic Verde River.

Rimrock and Cottonwood are neighboring communities known for their picturesque settings along the Verde River and the nearby Coconino National Forest. Visitors can enjoy fishing, kayaking, and hiking while immersing themselves in the area's natural beauty. Clarkdale is a historic mining town that offers a glimpse into Arizona's past. It is home to the Arizona Copper Art Museum and the Verde Canyon Railroad, a scenic train ride that takes visitors through breathtaking canyons. Perched on the side of Cleopatra Hill, Jerome is a charming hillside town known for its artistic community and well-preserved historic buildings. Visitors can explore galleries and shops and enjoy stunning views of the valley. The Village of Oak Creek, located just outside Sedona, offers a quieter alternative to the bustling tourist destination. Spectacular red rock formations surround it, providing access to hiking trails and outdoor activities. Sedona, the crown jewel of the third zone, is renowned for its red rock landscape, spiritual energy, and vibrant arts scene. It attracts visitors from around the world who come to enjoy the beauty of Oak Creek Canyon, hike the iconic Cathedral Rock, and experience the famous energy vortexes.

The fifth zone in Arizona's central region is a haven for nature lovers, history enthusiasts, and art aficionados alike, offering a delightful mix of natural wonders, cultural treasures, and a sense of serenity that makes it a captivating destination to explore and unwind.

1.Camp Verde

2.Rimrock

3.Cottonwood

4.Clarkdale

5.Jerome

6.Village of Oak Creek

7.Sedona

Sixth Zone

The sixth zone consists of Prescott, located in central Arizona. Here is a paragraph highlighting Prescott's key features:

Prescott, known as "Everybody's Hometown," is a charming city in Arizona's scenic central highlands. Steeped in history, Prescott is renowned for its rich Western heritage and Victorian architecture. The city's historic downtown, known as Whiskey Row, is lined with well-preserved buildings that once housed saloons and brothels during the Frontier era. Today, it is a vibrant hub of activity, offering boutiques, art galleries, restaurants, and lively entertainment venues. Prescott's pleasant climate and picturesque surroundings make it a popular destination for outdoor enthusiasts. The surrounding Prescott National Forest offers numerous hiking, mountain biking, camping, and horseback riding opportunities. Watson Lake and Lynx Lake, located nearby, provide scenic spots for fishing, boating, and picnicking. With its blend of history, natural beauty, and small-town charm, Prescott offers a delightful escape for visitors seeking a relaxed and authentic Arizona experience.

1.Prescott

Seventh Zone

ARIZONA BUCKET LIST

Arizona's seventh zone encompasses Flagstaff, Williams, Winslow, and the majestic Petrified Forest National Park. Flagstaff, situated amidst picturesque mountains, offers visitors a charming and lively atmosphere with its vibrant downtown, cultural events, and outdoor activities like hiking in the nearby Coconino National Forest. Williams, known as the "Gateway to the Grand Canyon," captivates visitors with its nostalgic Route 66 charm and as a departure point for the historic Grand Canyon Railway. Winslow, made famous by the Eagles' song "Take It Easy," invites travelers to stand on the corner at the dedicated park and explore its rich musical heritage. Finally, the awe-inspiring Petrified Forest National Park showcases mesmerizing landscapes, vibrant colors, and ancient fossilized wood, allowing visitors to immerse themselves in the region's remarkable natural wonders and fascinating geological history. The seventh zone presents a perfect blend of cultural charm and breathtaking natural beauty, offering a memorable experience for all who venture through its cities and national park.

1. Flagstaff

2. Williams

3. Winslow

4. Petrified Forest National Park

Eighth Zone

The eighth zone in Arizona encompasses the fascinating destinations of Hualapai and Oatman. Hualapai refers to both the Native American tribe and the region they inhabit. Nestled in the rugged landscapes of the Grand Canyon West, the Hualapai Reservation offers visitors a chance to explore the awe-inspiring beauty of the Grand Canyon from a unique perspective. The Hualapai Tribe operates the Grand Canyon Skywalk, a glass-bottomed bridge that extends over the canyon, providing breathtaking views and an exhilarating experience. Additionally, visitors can enjoy helicopter tours, whitewater rafting, and cultural experiences that showcase the rich heritage of the Hualapai people.

Conversely, Oatman is a charming historic mining town located along the iconic Route 66. Once a bustling gold mining center, Oatman has preserved its Wild West character, attracting visitors with its Old West ambiance, wooden boardwalks, and resident burros that freely roam the streets. Strolling through Oatman feels like stepping back in time, with its rustic buildings, saloons, and shops offering western-themed souvenirs. The town also hosts gunfights reenactments and lively events celebrating its colorful past.

The eighth zone in Arizona presents a captivating blend of Native American heritage, natural wonders, and nostalgic charm. From the awe-inspiring vistas of the Grand Canyon in the Hualapai region to the historic streets of Oatman, this zone offers visitors a chance to immerse themselves in the rich history and unique experiences that define Arizona's cultural and natural diversity.

1. Hualapai

2. Oatman

ARIZONA BUCKET LIST

Nineth Zone

Chinle, located in northeastern Arizona, is a captivating city that serves as the gateway to the awe-inspiring Canyon de Chelly National Monument. Nestled within the Navajo Nation, Chinle offers visitors a unique opportunity to immerse themselves in the region's rich cultural heritage. The towering sandstone cliffs and deep canyons of Canyon de Chelly have been home to Native American tribes for centuries, leaving behind a wealth of archaeological sites and stunning natural beauty. Exploring the canyon through guided tours or hiking its trails reveals ancient cliff dwellings, petroglyphs, and pictographs that offer a glimpse into the ancestral Puebloan and Navajo cultures. In addition to its archaeological treasures, Chinle offers opportunities to learn about the Navajo way of life and experience the vibrant traditions and arts of the Navajo people. From the interactive exhibits at the Navajo Nation Museum to the authentic crafts and jewelry available for purchase, visitors can engage with the rich tapestry of Navajo culture. With its captivating landscapes and deep cultural roots, Chinle is a destination that promises a genuinely enriching and immersive experience.

1.Chinle

Tenth Zone

Arizona's tenth zone comprises two remarkable destinations: Grand Canyon National Park and Supai. Grand Canyon National Park is one of the world's most iconic and awe-inspiring natural wonders. Spanning over 277 miles and reaching depths of over a mile, the Grand Canyon offers breathtaking vistas, layered rock formations, and a geological history that spans millions of years. Visitors can explore the park's numerous viewpoints, hike along its scenic trails, or embark on a thrilling whitewater rafting adventure along the Colorado River that carves through the canyon. The park also provides opportunities for camping, wildlife spotting, and stargazing, ensuring an unforgettable experience for nature enthusiasts.

Supai, located within the Grand Canyon, is a small Native American village belonging to the Havasupai Tribe. Accessible only by hiking or horseback, Supai offers a unique and remote experience for visitors. Its most famous attractions include the Havasu Falls, Mooney Falls, and Beaver Falls, renowned for their stunning turquoise waters cascading over deep red rock formations. The waterfalls and the surrounding Havasu Creek create a picturesque oasis amid the canyon, attracting adventurers and nature lovers worldwide. Camping permits are required to stay overnight in Supai, fully immersing visitors in this hidden gem's beauty.

The tenth zone in Arizona showcases the grandeur of the Grand Canyon National Park and the hidden beauty of Supai. Whether exploring the awe-inspiring vistas of the canyon or discovering the enchanting waterfalls and natural wonders of Supai, visitors to this zone are treated to unforgettable experiences that highlight the unparalleled beauty and diversity of Arizona's natural landscapes.

1.Grand Canyon National Park

2.Supai

ARIZONA BUCKET LIST

Eleventh Zone

The eleventh zone consists of the city of Page, located in northern Arizona. Here is a paragraph highlighting Page's key features:

Page, nestled in the stunning landscape of northern Arizona, is a city known for its incredible natural wonders and outdoor recreational opportunities. Situated near the southern shores of Lake Powell, Page offers a gateway to this vast reservoir renowned for its crystal-clear turquoise waters and majestic red rock cliffs. Visitors can enjoy boating, fishing, and swimming in the lake or leisurely cruise to explore its hidden coves and picturesque canyons. Another iconic attraction near Page is the breathtaking Antelope Canyon, a slot canyon famous for its beautiful light beams and intricate rock formations. Guided tours allow visitors to explore the narrow passages and capture stunning photographs. Additionally, the nearby Horseshoe Bend, a dramatic meander of the Colorado River, offers a mesmerizing panoramic view that will leave visitors in awe. Page is a haven for outdoor enthusiasts and nature lovers, offering a perfect blend of adventure and natural beauty.

1.Page

Twelfth Zone

The twelfth zone consists of the city of Tuba City, located in the northern part of Arizona. Here is a paragraph highlighting Tuba City's key features:

Tuba City is a vibrant community situated in the heart of the Navajo Nation, offering a glimpse into the rich culture and traditions of the Navajo people. This city serves as a hub for exploring the natural wonders of the surrounding area, including the nearby Navajo National Monument. Here, visitors can witness ancient cliff dwellings and experience the profound history of the Ancestral Puebloans. Tuba City is known for its annual Western Navajo Fair, which celebrates Navajo culture through traditional music, dance, rodeos, and arts and crafts. Visitors can immerse themselves in the unique Navajo cuisine and arts scene, with opportunities to purchase authentic jewelry, pottery, and textiles. Tuba City is an inviting destination for those seeking an authentic and immersive experience in the rich heritage of the Navajo Nation.

1.Tuba City

Thirteenth Zone

The thirteenth zone comprises the iconic Monument Valley, a place of timeless beauty and captivating landscapes. Located on the Arizona-Utah border, Monument Valley is renowned for its towering sandstone buttes, mesas, and dramatic red rock formations that have become symbols of the American West. The vast, open desert expanse dotted with monolithic rock structures creates a breathtaking panorama featured in countless movies, television shows, and photographs. Visitors to Monument Valley can embark on scenic drives, guided tours, or even horseback rides to explore the mesmerizing terrain and soak in the majestic views. The area holds deep cultural significance for the Navajo Nation, and visitors can learn about the rich Navajo traditions, folklore, and history through interactions with the local Navajo guides and at the visitor center. Monument Valley offers an awe-inspiring experience that captures the essence of the Southwest's natural beauty and Native American heritage.

1.Monument Valley

Fourteenth Zone

The fourteenth zone consists of the city of Payson, nestled in the picturesque Mogollon Rim region of Arizona. Payson is a charming mountain town known for its scenic beauty and outdoor recreational opportunities. Surrounded by the breathtaking Tonto National Forest, visitors to Payson can immerse themselves in the splendor of nature. The area boasts numerous hiking trails, including the famous Horton Creek Trail and the breathtaking Tonto Natural Bridge, one of the world's largest natural travertine bridges. Fishing enthusiasts can enjoy casting their lines in the nearby lakes and rivers, such as the picturesque Woods Canyon Lake or the mighty Tonto Creek. Payson also hosts various outdoor festivals and events throughout the year, showcasing the local arts, crafts, and culture. With its tranquil mountain setting, abundant wildlife, and opportunities for outdoor adventures, Payson is a haven for those seeking a peaceful retreat in the heart of Arizona's natural wonders.

1.Payson

MAP

We have devised an interactive map that includes all destinations described in the book. You can easily plan your itinerary with this map, saving you time and effort.
Additionally, the map is compatible with Google Maps.

Scan the following QR or type in the provided link to receive it:

https://jo.my/azbucketlistform

You will receive an email with links to access the Interactive Map. If you do not see our email, please look for it in spam or another section of your inbox.

In case you have any problems, you can write us at **TravelBucketList@becrepress.com.**

Made in the USA
Las Vegas, NV
09 November 2024

11387354R00066